Remodelling & Repairing Kitchen Cabinets

Remodelling & Repairing Kitchen Cabinets

Sam Allen

 Sterling Publishing Co., Inc.   New York

Edited by Laurel Ornitz

Library of Congress Cataloging-in-Publication Data

Allen, Sam.
   Remodelling & repairing kitchen cabinets / Sam Allen.
     p. cm.
   Includes index.
   ISBN 0-8069-6720-X (pbk.)
    1. Kitchen cabinets—Remodeling.   2. Kitchen cabinets—Repairing.
I. Title. II. Title: Remodelling and repairing kitchen cabinets.
TT197.A453   1988
684.1′6—dc19

                                                   88-11717
                                                      CIP

Copyright © 1988 by Sam Allen
Published by Sterling Publishing Co., Inc.
Two Park Avenue, New York, N.Y. 10016
Distributed in Canada by Oak Tree Press Ltd.
℅ Canadian Manda Group, P.O. Box 920, Station U
Toronto, Ontario, Canada M8Z 5P9
Distributed in the United Kingdom by Blandford Press
Link House, West Street, Poole, Dorset BH15 1LL, England
Distributed in Australia by Capricorn Ltd.
P.O. Box 665, Lane Cove, NSW 2066
Manufactured in the United States of America
Sterling ISBN 0-8069-6720-X Paper

Contents

Introduction

Today many homeowners are willing to use their own labor to increase the value of their homes. Besides an increased equity, they also get a sense of pride in their homes that comes from doing the work themselves.

Kitchen cabinets are prime candidates for do-it-yourself repair and remodelling. A kitchen make-over increases the value of a home and improves its day-to-day livability. If you are willing to invest your time, you can probably do the job for less than a third of the cost you would normally pay a contractor. Part of the savings comes from reusing materials. Since salvaging old material takes increased labor, it is usually impractical for a contractor; but when you are providing the labor yourself, you can take advantage of the savings. Before you tackle a major cabinet-remodelling job, you need to determine whether the existing cabinets are worth the effort. If the cabinets are poorly built and made from cheap materials, you will be better off installing new cabinets. But, if the existing cabinets are basically sound and built from quality materials, you can reuse most of the materials and save a lot of money.

Cabinets built before the mid-1960s were usually custom-made. In most cases they are plain-looking and without much style, but they are usually built from quality materials, such as ¾"-thick birch plywood, fir plywood, or solid pine lumber. These cabinets are perfect for remodelling since you can easily update them and add some style. After the mid-'60s, factory-made cabinets were being used in most new homes. If these cabinets are made from quality materials, then they can also be easily updated. However, some inexpensive homes have very cheap cabinets, built from ⅜" particle board, with hollow-core doors; these cabinets usually require so much repair and new material that buying new cabinets will probably be better in the long run.

If you are happy with the present style of your cabinets, then you may

Illus. 1. You can update or change the style of kitchen cabinets by removing the doors and drawer fronts and then modifying them or replacing them with new ones.

only need to do a few simple repairs to make them like new again. The first chapter of this book provides instructions for some of the most frequently needed types of cabinet repairs.

When the cabinets are in need of more than a few simple repairs or you want to change the look or layout of the kitchen, then it's time to remodel. The remaining chapters cover a variety of remodelling techniques. You can achieve a dramatic change in the look of your cabinets simply by changing the doors and drawer fronts (see Illus. 1). In many cases, you can reuse the existing materials and add decorative features to change the style. Chapter 2 covers decorative treatments, such as adding a routed pattern to the door front (Illus. 2), or adding a moulding to imitate a panel door (Illus. 3).

You can give the cabinets an entirely new look by covering the existing doors with plastic laminates (Illus. 4), which are available in a wide range of colors and patterns. Because they are extremely durable, plastic laminates are especially useful when the cabinets will receive hard use and

Illus. 2. One way to change the style of flat plywood doors is to rout a decorative design in the face.

Illus. 3. An applied moulding is used on these doors to make them look like panel doors.

frequent cleaning. Chapter 3 tells you how to cover old doors with plastic laminate.

When the existing doors can't be adapted to the style you want or the materials aren't worth reusing, then you can construct new doors and drawer fronts and apply them to the existing cabinet carcass. Chapter 4 gives instructions on making several types of new doors and drawer fronts (Illus. 5).

Chapter 5 describes different types of cabinet hardware and how they are installed. Replacing worn-out or out-of-date hardware can bring old cabinets back to life.

You can further modify existing cabinets by replacing old shelves with

Illus. 4. You can apply plastic laminate to old doors to update the style and give them a durable surface.

adjustable shelves (Chapter 6), making new drawers (Chapter 7), or making structural changes (Chapter 8).

In Chapter 9, you can follow a typical project from start to finish. This chapter shows how all of the elements come together in an actual remodelling job.

Whether you choose to make a few repairs or do a total remodelling job, you will feel the satisfaction and pride that comes from doing the work yourself. But don't let an accident mar that enjoyment. Follow the manufacturer's safety instructions for the tools and materials you use. In some of the photos in this book, guards have been removed from certain tools to show the operations more clearly; *but when you are using power tools, be sure to leave all guards in place.*

A major kitchen-remodelling job takes a lot of time, so it's a good idea to do the work when you have a block of time available, such as a vacation or a leave from work. That way the kitchen won't be disrupted

Illus. 5. New cabinet doors can totally change the look of a kitchen. Panel doors, as shown here, are just one type of new door you can make.

over a long period of time. If you can't devote a block of time to the project, consider making new doors since this option can be done in your spare time without disrupting the kitchen. Build the doors before removing anything from the existing cabinets; then, when all of the new doors are finished, you can install them over a weekend or two.

1
Repairs

Kitchen cabinets probably receive more day-to-day use than any other part of a house, so it's not unusual that they frequently are in need of repair. Hinges loosen or wear out, drawer guides wear, joints loosen or break, and leaking pipes can cause water damage. However, with a few simple hand tools, you can usually fix all of these problems yourself.

HINGES

Every time you open a door the hinge wears a little. After many years of use, cabinet hinges can wear out. The signs are not always obvious, but when doors don't fit as well as they should and they stick or fail to close or if the catches no longer line up, then the hinges may be due for replacement (Illus. 6). To check the hinges, open the door and grab the edge. Try to move the door up and down. If there is more than a tiny amount of play in the hinges, they are worn (Illus. 7). Hinges come in many types and styles, but you can almost always find an exact replacement at a well-stocked hardware dealer's. If you are only changing the hinges on a few frequently used doors, then it's best to try for an exact replacement. However, if you need to replace many hinges, you may want to consider changing to a more modern style. (Chapter 5 gives directions for changing to a different type of hinge.)

When hinges wear out prematurely, there may be other factors besides normal use causing this to happen. Check to see that the hinges were correctly installed. If the hinges bind, they will wear out too soon. In some cases, the hinges used may not be strong enough to carry the weight of larger doors. Adding a third hinge in the middle will usually solve this problem, or you can switch to heavy-duty hinges. Loose screws on one hinge can lead to abnormal wear on another hinge. If the screws on the top hinge are loose, then the lower hinge will be carrying more of the weight of the door. It may also be flexing as it moves, causing metal fatigue that can result in a broken hinge. If you tighten loose

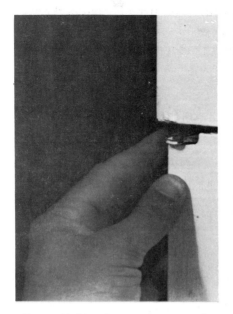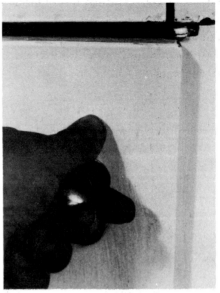

Illus. 6 (left). After many years of use, cabinet hinges can wear out. This hinge has worn to the point where the edge of the door no longer lines up with the drawer above it. Illus. 7 (right). You can test for worn hinges by lifting the pull side of the door. This door has ¼" of play, indicating a very worn hinge.

screws as soon as you notice them, you can save yourself a major repair job later.

Screw holes may become enlarged to the point where the screw no longer can be tightened. When this happens, the holes are said to be stripped. There are several ways to deal with stripped screw holes. One of the simplest is to glue a sliver of wood into the hole and then reinsert the screw after the glue is dry. This will work if the screw isn't under a lot of strain, but usually the problem soon reoccurs because often the screw *is* under a lot of strain or it wouldn't have stripped in the first place. A stripped screw hole may indicate that the screw isn't large enough to handle the weight; replacing the screw with the next larger diameter can solve the problem. If the wood is thick enough, using a longer screw is also a good way to solve the problem.

Screws don't hold very well in the end grain of solid lumber or in the edge of plywood or particle board. In both cases, you can increase the holding power by drilling the hole out and gluing in a section of hardwood dowel. In Illus. 8, the method shown in "A" works fairly well even though the screw is driven into the end grain of the dowel, but the method shown in "B" is better because the screw is driven into the side of the dowel. When you replace a hinge that is attached to end grain or the edge of plywood or particle board, get the type that has an ear that bends around the side of the wood to provide screw attachment to the side.

When normal measures fail to keep a screw from stripping out of the wood, you can use a brass insert that has wood screw threads on the outside and machine threads on the inside. Drill the hole large enough to fit the insert and screw the insert into the wood; then use a machine screw to attach the hinge to the insert.

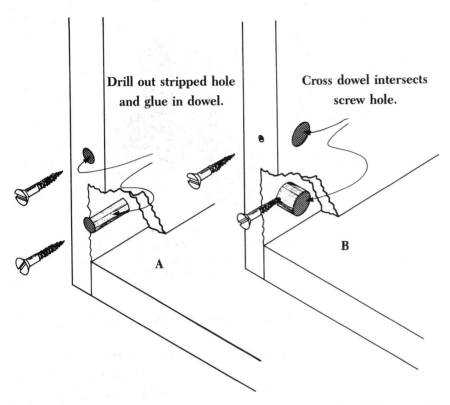

Drill out stripped hole and glue in dowel.

Cross dowel intersects screw hole.

A

B

Illus. 8. When a screw hole is stripped, you can repair it by drilling the hole larger and gluing a dowel in place (as shown in "A") or by drilling a hole in the side to intersect the hole and gluing a dowel in at a right angle to the screw (as shown in "B"). The second method is stronger, but it may not always be practical.

CATCHES

Catches are another type of hardware that frequently causes a problem on older cabinets. If a door won't stay closed, the catch is most likely at fault; however, a warped or binding door can prevent a catch from working properly.

To find out if the door is binding, gently push the door shut. If you start to feel resistance before the door is fully shut, then the door is probably binding on the hinge edge. Look at the hinge as you shut the door. If it bends or moves, the door edge is probably touching the face frame before the door is fully shut. To make sure, slightly loosen the hinge screws. If the door now shuts normally, you have found the problem. You can sometimes take care of this by placing thin paper or cardboard shims between the hinge and the face frame before retightening the screws. If this doesn't help, remove the door and plane a little from the edge on the hinge side.

When the fault is in the catch, the problem may be very obvious, such as a broken or missing catch (Illus. 9). In these situations, the remedy is simply to replace the catch. But sometimes the problem is not so obvious. If the catch doesn't line up properly, it won't work, but it's hard to tell with the door open. On a two-door cabinet, leave one of the doors open and look inside as you close the other door. Catches have slotted screw holes to allow for adjustment. If you see that the catch isn't properly lined up, loosen the screws and move the catch until it lines up correctly and then retighten the screws (Illus. 10). On a single-door cabinet, you may not be able to see inside as you close the door. In this case, it's best to adjust the catch by using the same method used to install a new catch. Remove the latch plate from the door and place it on the catch in the correct position. Loosen the catch and move it to the farthest-out position and retighten the screws. Now, firmly close the door. The latch plate has a small point that will make a mark on the door; find the mark and then reinstall the plate so that the point fits into the mark. Next, close the door and note how much of a gap there is between the door and the face frame; then open the door and adjust the catch back to the point where the door will fit correctly. (See Chapter 5 for more details.)

Many newer cabinets eliminate the need for catches by using self-closing hinges. However, if the spring mechanism in the hinge breaks, the door won't stay closed. Replacing the hinge will solve the problem;

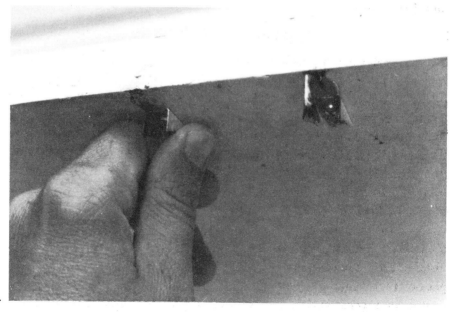

Illus. 9. When a door won't stay closed, broken catches may be causing the problem.

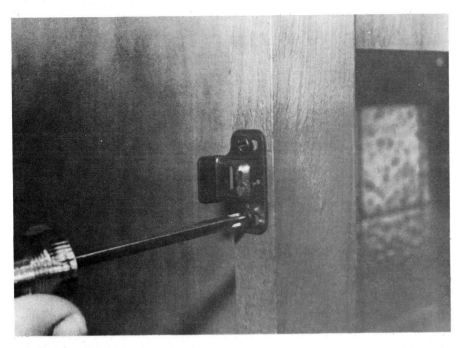

Illus. 10. Most catches have slotted holes to allow you to adjust the catch slightly without moving the screws.

or if the hinge functions correctly except for the closing portion, you may want to add a magnetic or friction catch to hold the door shut. Binding along the hinge edge of the door is more troublesome with self-closing hinges. Even a slight amount of binding can prevent the door from closing correctly. It may be necessary to reposition the hinge to solve a binding problem. Because the amount of movement will be slight, the old screw holes will tend to draw the screws back to their original positions; therefore, when repositioning the hinge, it's best to enlarge the old holes with a ¼"-diameter drill and glue a section of ¼" hardwood dowel into them.

DRAWER GUIDES

Drawer guides can be made of wood or they can be commercially made metal units. The most common problem with wood guides is wear. Wood rubbing against wood eventually wears down the guides to the point where the drawer will no longer operate correctly. With the drawer removed, you may even notice a small amount of sawdust as evidence of the wear (Illus. 11). Extensive wear may lead to a broken drawer guide (Illus. 12). The solution to this problem is to make a new wood guide using a table saw with a dado blade or to replace the guide with a commercial metal type.

When the side of the drawer is used as a guide, it may wear down the frame that it rests on (Illus. 13). One way to solve this problem is to install plastic guides for the drawer to rest on; made of a long-wearing plastic, these guides will make the drawer operate with less friction. Chisel out a recess in the frame to accommodate the plastic guide (Illus.

14), and then attach the guide with tacks or staples (Illus. 15). You can also install small rollers, such as the ones shown in Illus. 16. These have a flange to attach to the face frame, and the roller fits behind. If you don't want to use one of these commercial guides, use a chisel or file to square up the worn section of the original guide and glue in a strip of new wood (Illus. 17). Use hardwood for the longest life, and rub the guide with paraffin to lubricate it.

Metal drawer guides have rollers to help prevent wear, so they will function for a long time. If the rollers wear out, the best option is to replace the entire guide. Usually the guide itself is all right, although sometimes it comes loose from its mounting. If the screws are stripped, use the techniques described for hinges on page 12 to remedy the problem. The type of center guide shown in Illus. 18 is mounted to the back of the cabinet and the front face frame. In many cabinets the guide is attached with staples. If the staples come loose, replace them with

Illus. 11. This pile of sawdust is evidence of the wear that can occur when wood rubs against wood in a drawer guide.

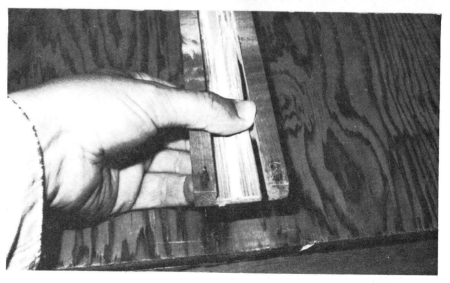

Illus. 12. This guide wore so thin that it eventually split.

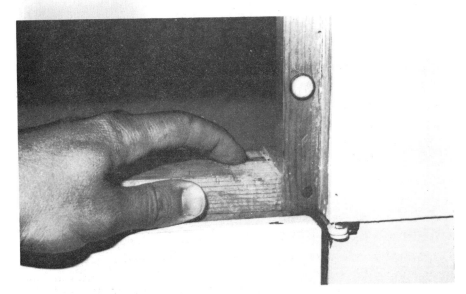

Illus. 13. Wear on the frame, as shown here, will cause the drawer to sit lower in its opening; eventually the drawer may hit the door below and make it difficult to open or close.

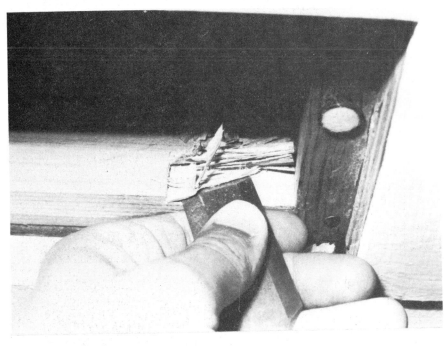

Illus. 14. Chisel out a recess for the plastic guide to a depth that will put the top of the guide flush with the original unworn surface of the frame.

screws (Illus. 19). In some very inexpensive cabinets, the guide will be stapled directly to the hardboard back without a wood support block. For the best repair, add a block similar to the one used in Illus. 19. You will have to remove the guides and use a hacksaw to cut ¾" from the rear of each guide to allow for the thickness of the support block. Then reinstall the guides with screws.

The rear roller that is attached to the drawer is also placed under a lot of strain with this type of guide. When the drawers are made of a soft wood, the wood screws holding the roller will usually strip out after a few years. Instead of replacing these screws with other wood screws, use

Illus. 15 (left). Install the plastic guide with tacks or staples. This guide has a disc roller to decrease friction, whereas other types are solid plastic. Illus. 16 (right). This type of roller can also be used to reduce friction between the sides of the drawer and the face frame.

machine screws and nuts. Drill the screw holes all the way through the back (Illus. 20). Replace the roller and secure it with machine screws and nuts (Illus. 21). Use washers to keep the screws from pulling through the wood, and put a daub of liquid lock washer or silicone glue on the screw threads to keep the nuts from loosening.

Roller guides make a drawer slide in and out so freely that it is easy to damage the drawer by slamming it shut. Usually the front of the drawer

Illus. 17. Instead of using a commercial guide, you can replace the worn area with a strip of hardwood glued in place.

hits the face frame, eventually causing the front to pull loose from the rest of the drawer. When this happens, the front needs to be reattached to the drawer and a stop needs to be installed to prevent it from happening again.

Drawers are constructed in several ways. The type of drawer construction determines the best way of reattaching a drawer front that has been knocked loose. The type shown in Illus. 22 uses a false front attached with screws. This is probably the easiest type to repair. The old screw

Illus. 18. This type of metal guide is mounted to the middle of the face frame and the back of the cabinet. Plastic rollers on the face frame reduce the friction.

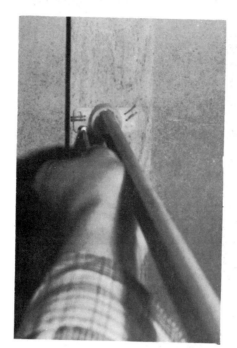

Illus. 19 (left). The rear attachment point is often the weak link with this type of guide. If the mount is stapled in place, you can reinforce it with screws. This mount is attached to a ¾" wood support. Illus. 20 (right). The screw holes in the back of the drawer are another problem area with this type of guide. To repair a stripped hole, first drill the hole all the way through.

holes will be stripped, so drill new ones close to the original positions and reattach the front with screws.

When a drawer front with a tongue-and-lap type of joint (Illus. 23) breaks, the tongue usually breaks off. Add dowels, as shown in Illus. 24, to reinforce the joint when you glue it back together. When the joint is so badly broken that it can't be repaired with dowels, you can still salvage the drawer by adding a backing board. Glue the broken parts of the drawer back together, and then add a board behind the original front, as shown in Illus. 25. Use screws through the backing board to attach it to the front, and then screw through the drawer sides into the backing board.

In high-quality commercial cabinets, dovetail joints are used to attach the front. These joints are stronger and less likely to break; but when they do, you can repair them by adding a backing board.

Once you have repaired the drawer, add a stop that will take the strain off the drawer front when the drawer is slammed. To do this, you need to be able to see the back of the drawer when it is closed. You can usually open a cabinet door below or remove another drawer to see the back. Attach a block of wood to the sides of the cabinet with glue and screws directly in back of the drawer sides so that the rear of the drawer will hit

Illus. 21. After drilling through the back of the drawer, you can reinstall the roller using machine screws and nuts. Use a washer on the inside of the drawer to keep the screw head from pulling through the wood.

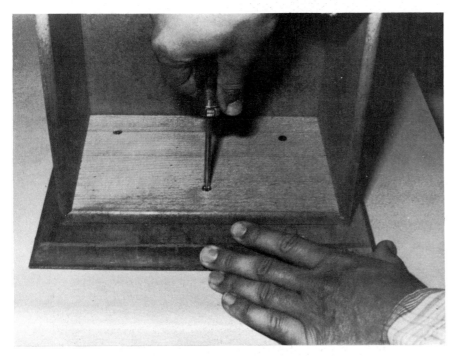

Illus. 22. This type of drawer has a false front attached with screws. If the screw holes become stripped, you can change the position of the holes slightly and reinstall the screws.

these blocks when the drawer is fully closed. Instead of the drawer front, the blocks will now take the impact of the slammed drawer.

Illus. 23 (left). This drawer front is attached directly to the sides with a tongue-and-lap joint. When this joint breaks, the tongue usually breaks off. Illus. 24 (right). When you glue a drawer front back on the drawer, dowels can be added to reinforce the joint.

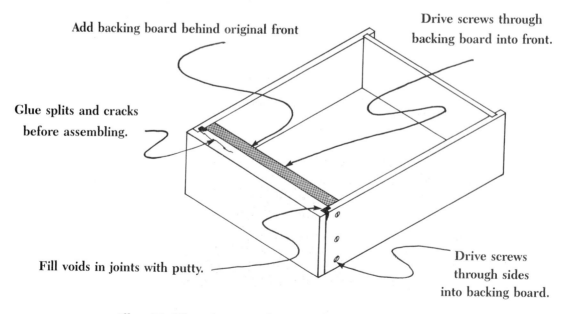

Add backing board behind original front

Drive screws through backing board into front.

Glue splits and cracks before assembling.

Fill voids in joints with putty.

Drive screws through sides into backing board.

Illus. 25. When the original joint is damaged beyond repair, you can still salvage the drawer by adding a backing board behind the original front.

BROKEN JOINTS

Panel doors are made from individual parts joined together to make a frame around a panel. The joints on panel doors are placed under a lot of strain when the doors are opened and closed, particularly when the door binds or it is slammed shut or pulled open too far. The result can be a broken joint, usually on the hinge side (Illus. 26). The door in Illus. 27 is typical of many commercially made panel doors. It uses a stub-tenon joint. This type of joint is easy to mass-produce, but it doesn't have the strength of the traditional haunched tenon.

If you simply glue the joint back together, it will likely break again; so you need to add some additional reinforcement. You can use screws or

Illus. 26. On the hinge side of a panel door, a lot of strain is placed on the joint between the rail and stile. The type of breakage shown here often results when too much strain is applied to the joint.

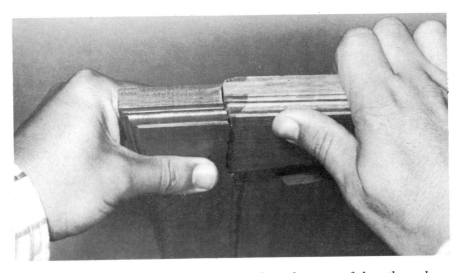

Illus. 27. Stub-tenon joints tend to break along the grain of the stile at the end of the tenon.

nails to reinforce the joint, but you should drill pilot holes to avoid splitting the stile. If you use screws, 2½″ No. 8 dry-wall screws are best. Drill in from the outside edge of the stile through the joint. Counterbore the screw heads below the surface and hide them with a dowel plug. When the appearance of the back of the door is unimportant, you can reinforce the joint with a metal mending plate screwed to the rear of the door.

When you are repairing a broken joint, you'll get the strongest and best-looking joint if you use blind dowels (Illus. 28). The stile must be completely removed from the door to do this. If only one joint is broken, saw through the remaining joint with a saw that makes a very thin kerf or split the joint with a chisel; then add dowels to both joints. Use a dowelling jig to position the holes, and stop drilling before the holes break through the edge of the board. Spread glue on the dowel and both

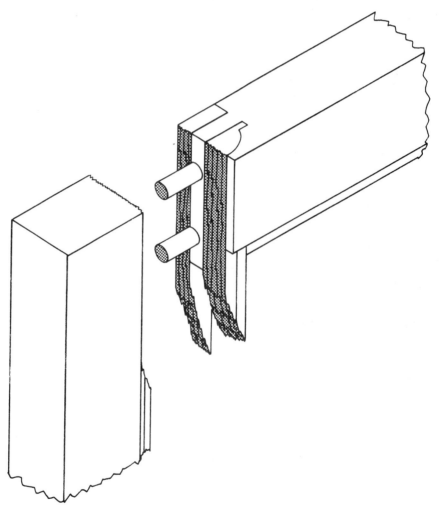

Illus. 28. Blind dowels can be used to reinforce a broken joint with no visible change to the outward appearance.

surfaces of the joint before assembling. Don't allow any glue to get into the groove for the panel. The panel must be free to float in the frame; if the panel isn't free, it will probably crack as a result of shrinkage or swelling due to changes in humidity. Use bar clamps to pull the joints together. Use at least three clamps. Place the middle clamp with the bar on the opposite face of the door. This will equalize the force and prevent the rail from twisting in the direction of the bars. When the glue has set, remove the clamps and carefully scrape off any excess glue with a sharp chisel. If there are small gaps in the surface of the joint or scratches in the finish, rub a putty stick over them.

WATER DAMAGE

Cabinets below the sink are particularly prone to water damage. Even if the pipes don't leak, they may sweat, and spilled water from the sink can run down the face of the cabinet.

Delaminated Plies   Constant exposure to water may cause the plies in plywood to come apart; this is called delamination. If it is not too severe, you can glue the plies back together. Use a water-resistant glue. Force the plies apart by inserting a chisel into the crack. Use a thin strip of wood to spread the glue inside the crack. Remove the chisel and press the plies together several times to further distribute the glue. The success of this repair depends on getting the glue as thoroughly distributed in the delaminated area as possible. Now, clamp the plies tightly together and let the glue set.

Buckled Face Plies   When the face plies delaminate, they tend to buckle up, creating a wavy surface on the board. Use a sharp knife to slit the ply at the buckle and force some glue under the ply; then place a cloth over the area and use a steam iron to flatten out the wood. Immediately place a piece of wax paper over the area, followed by a flat board. Clamp the board in place and allow the glue to set.

Replacing a Shelf   When a shelf has been damaged by water, it usually sags and is difficult to repair; so the best way to remedy the problem is to replace the shelf. Particle-board shelves are particularly prone to this type of damage. If you are replacing a particle-board shelf, use plywood or lumber for the replacement to avoid a reoccurrence. If the shelves are adjustable, it is a simple matter to remove the old shelf and install a new one; but when the shelves are permanently attached, the procedure is more involved.

Shelves are usually either attached with cleats or in dadoes. If cleats are used, remove them with a pry bar and take out the shelf. Then cut a new shelf and install it. If the cleats are damaged, replace them; otherwise, the cleats can be reused. The most difficult type of shelf to replace is the type that uses dadoes. To remove the shelf, use a sabre saw or a handsaw to cut the shelf in half. Bend the halves down to loosen them in the joints, and pull them out of the dadoes. Watch the wood around the dadoes for signs of splitting. If the wood starts to split, press against the area with a block of wood to help keep the sides from splintering. After the shelf has been removed, there will usually be some nails left protruding from the dado. Pounding the nails back out will usually cause damage to the other side of the board. If the face is visible, it is better to pull the heads through from the dado side by grasping the nails with a pair of pliers. Place a block of wood next to the nail. Grip the nail close to the wood and bend the nail until the edge of the pliers jaw rests against the block. Push the pliers handle towards the dado to pry out the nail (Illus. 29). You may need to regrip the nail several times before it is completely out.

Illus. 29. Pliers can be used to pull the nails through from the inside after you have removed a shelf. Use a piece of wood to protect the area from any marks left by the pliers.

If the shelf is at least 3′ long, there will be enough spring in the board to get the shelf back into the dadoes. Spread glue into the dado and put one end of the shelf in the dado with the other end resting above the dado. Place one hand in the middle of the shelf against the underside and the other hand on the upper side near the end that is not yet in a dado. Push up in the middle and down on the end. The board will bend enough to allow the end to slip into the dado. Nail through the dado from the opposite face to reinforce the joint.

If the shelf is short, then there probably won't be enough spring in it to get it into a dado using the method just described. In this case, install cleats in the dado (Illus. 30). The cleats should extend about ¾″ past the side. Place the shelf on top of the cleats and attach the cleats to the underside of the shelf with screws.

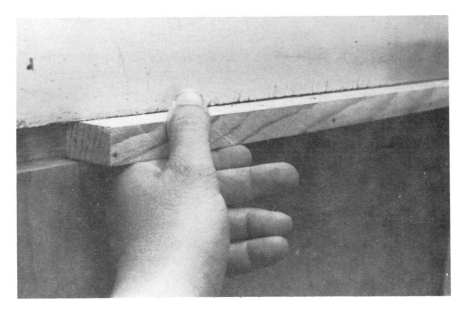

Illus. 30. You can install cleats in the dado to support the new shelf if you can't get a new full-length shelf into the old dadoes.

When the bottom shelf on a cabinet is water-damaged, sometimes you can merely cover it with a new piece of wood. You can get by without removing the bottom shelf since it's supported by the base and won't sag as much as an unsupported shelf. Usually the problem is that the face plies of the plywood delaminate, creating a rough splintery surface. If the shelf is solid otherwise, then you can cover it with a piece of ⅛" or ¼" hardboard to achieve a smooth surface. Use tempered hardboard for water resistance. Strip off all of the loose plies from the original shelf. Trim the hardboard to fit over it and around the stile if necessary. If there is a center stile between two doors, then you may not be able to get the hardboard into the cabinet in one piece. In that case, cut the hardboard in half so that the joint will fall in the center of the middle stile. Use a caulking gun to spread panel adhesive on the shelf and set the hardboard in place. Use a few finishing nails around the edges and at the joint to hold the hardboard down while the glue sets. Placing some heavy weights on the hardboard will also help hold it down as the glue sets.

2

Decorative Treatments

You can decorate the flat plywood doors and drawer fronts commonly found on older cabinets in several ways to add a new look to your kitchen (Illus. 31). Designs can be cut into the surface of these doors and drawer fronts with a table saw or router, mouldings can be applied to the surfaces, and sheets of woven cane can be applied to the doors.

Illus. 31. These plywood doors are typical of the doors found on many older cabinets. This chapter shows several ways to give them a new look.

CUT DESIGNS

You can cut several types of designs into the surface of a door or drawer front. When the design consists of straight lines, you can use a table saw; when it consists of curved cuts, you'll need to use a router and a special guide.

One of the simplest designs you can make is shown in Illus. 32; it is a series of grooves, cut with a standard blade on the table saw. Use the rip fence to guide the cut. The cut should be very shallow so that it just scores the face ply of the plywood. The cuts can be vertical or horizontal. The grooves make the doors look as if they are made from tongue-and-

Illus. 32. The grooves cut into the face of these doors make the doors look as if they were made from tongue-and-groove lumber instead of plywood. The cleats at the top and bottom were made from ¼" plywood glued into a rabbet. The edges were covered with veneer tape after the cleats were in place.

groove lumber. The finished look can range from country to modern. For more of a country look, add cleats, as shown in Illus. 33. In this case, the cleat is made from ¼" plywood and set into a rabbet along the bottom edge of the door, but the cleats can also be applied to the surface of the door. Cleats applied in a Z- or X-pattern can be very effective.

When you want a wider groove, use a dado blade. The dado blade will tend to chip the face of the door more than a standard blade, so place masking tape over the areas to be cut to avoid any chipping. The cuts can be made up to ⅛" deep. Deeper cuts may weaken the door.

A router can be used in a similar manner to decorate doors and drawers. With the router, you can make an even better imitation of tongue-and-groove lumber because you can use a V-groove bit or a core-box bit, which makes a round bottom cut.

You can make a simple guide for your router out of scrap wood (Illus. 34). Start by making a mark on one of the boards that clamp to the edge of the door to indicate the point where you want to align it with the corner of the door. Next, measure the distance from the middle of the router bit to the edge of the router base. Measure this distance from the starting mark and make another mark; then from that point on, mark off the distance between grooves. Place the two side boards next to each other and use a square to transfer the marks to the second board. Now, clamp the side boards to the door using bar clamps. Align the starting mark on the boards with the edge of the door. Place the clamps under the door and keep the jaws below the surface of the board so that they

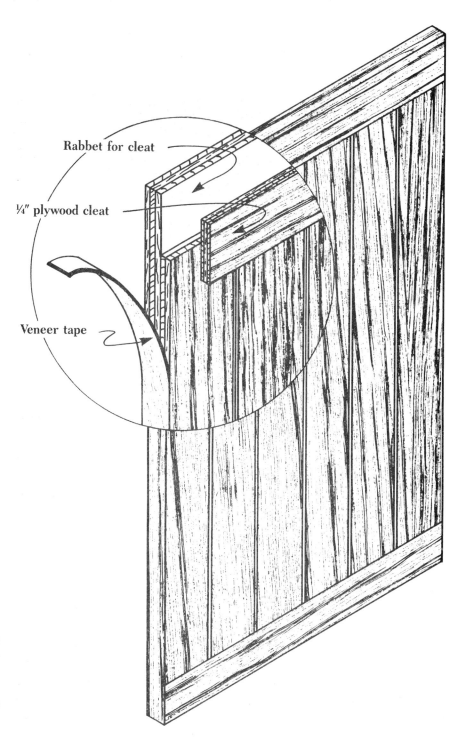

Rabbet for cleat

¼″ plywood cleat

Veneer tape

Illus. 33. This drawing shows how the cleats fit into the door. Use a table saw or router to make the rabbet. It will take several passes over the dado blade to make a rabbet this wide.

won't interfere with the router. Next, place a strip of ¼″ hardboard with a good straight edge across the door and align it with the second set of marks. Use small C-clamps or the spring-type clamps shown in Illus. 34 to hold the hardboard guide in place. Make the cut with the router base rubbing against the hardboard guide; then move the guide strip to the next mark and make another cut.

This same guide can be used to make diagonal cuts. Just lay out the marks on the side boards at the desired angle and clamp the guide strip

Illus. 34. You can use this setup to make a series of grooves with a router. Since the boards clamped to the edges of the door have the guide locations marked on them, you don't need to lay out each door separately.

diagonally across the door. The side boards will need to be longer than the door in order to make all of the cuts without moving them.

Cuts made with the router are easier to start and stop than those made on the table saw, so this gives you more freedom in the design you choose. Some of the designs you can use are shown in Illus. 35.

It will be helpful if you use a thicker guide board for the router base to ride against. Hold the base against the guide and align the bit with the starting point with the bit raised off the surface. Start the router before lowering it into the wood. At the end of the cut, stop the router and wait until the bit stops turning before you lift the router from the work.

The doors in Illus. 36 were made with a commercial router guide. This type of guide can be used to make several different corner shapes and arched tops. There are two types of commercial router guides: heavy-duty and standard-duty. The heavy-duty type is used by cabinet shops. The router is mounted on a platform that rides on bearings and a

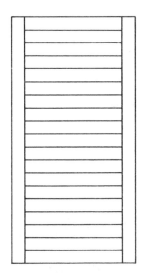
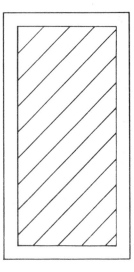
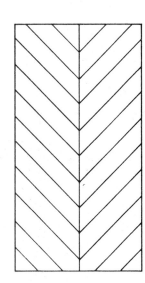

Illus. 35. Several designs that can be made with the router.

special track. The standard-duty type, shown in Illus. 37, has four aluminum guide rails, which can be adjusted to any-size door or drawer front. The corner templates are interchangeable, and several designs are available. A guide bushing fits into the router base around the bit. The bushing rubs against the guide. Many types of bits can be used with this guide to produce various effects, ranging from a simple straight or V groove to a special wide ogee bit used to imitate a panel door (Illus. 38).

The cut will expose the interior plies of the plywood. Depending on the type of plywood and the design of the router bit, the effect may or may not be desirable. If you like the exposed plies, you can finish the

Illus. 36. Using a special router guide, you can produce designs like this.

Illus. 37. This guide can be adjusted to fit many sizes of doors and drawer fronts. Since the corner templates are interchangeable, a number of different designs can be made.

Illus. 38. Special router bits are available that can be used to produce this type of cut as well as many others.

routed area with stain and varnish. If the pattern of the plies is not to your liking, then use paint to finish the routed area. You can create a wide range of effects by using matching or contrasting colors to finish the groove.

CANE PANELLING

The router can also be used to prepare a door to receive a cane panel (Illus. 39). Cane comes in prewoven sheets, in both modern and traditional weave (Illus. 40–42). The cane is held in place by a reed spline that fits into a groove in the door. Use a router with a straight bit to make the groove. The size of the bit depends on the size of the spline you buy; splines are available in ³⁄₁₆″ to ⁵⁄₁₆″ widths with ⁷⁄₃₂″ to ⁵⁄₁₆″ depths.

You can use a router guide, such as the one shown in Illus. 37, to make

Illus. 39. A cane panel can be added to a flat plywood door to give it a completely new look.

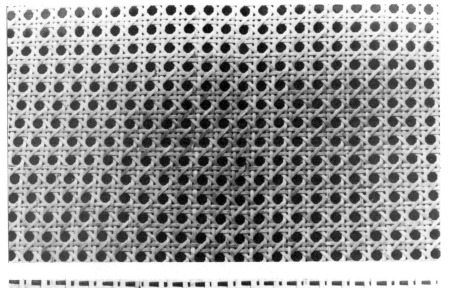

Illus. 40. Machine-woven cane is available in several styles. This is conventional weave.

Illus. 41. This style of cane is called modern open weave.

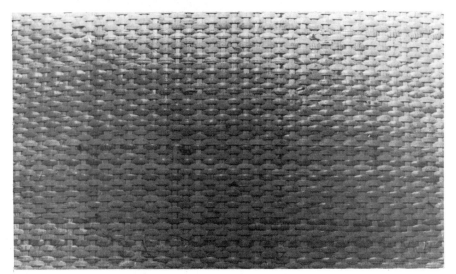

Illus. 42. This style is modern closed weave.

the groove for the spline. Any of the decorative corner shapes or an arched top can be used. If you choose square corners, then you can simply use a router fence to guide the cut (Illus. 43).

Use scissors to cut the cane to size. Allow for at least a ¼″ overhang past the outside edge of the groove (Illus. 44). Soak the cane in water until it is thoroughly wet and pliable. As the cane dries, it will shrink, giving it a very tight, smooth fit.

Next, cut the reed spline to size with a sharp knife or a fine-toothed saw. You can use a mitre box to make mitre joints at the corners. Try the spline in the grooves to check the joints, and then remove it. Spread aliphatic resin woodworking glue in the groove. The sides and bottom of the groove should be evenly coated. A soldering-flux brush is useful for

Illus. 43. The cane is applied in a groove. You can use a router fence to guide the router when you're using square corners, as shown here. To cut decorative corner designs, use the special guide shown in Illus. 37.

Illus. 44. Use scissors to cut the cane to size. Allow at least a ¼" overhang past the groove.

spreading the glue. Place the wet cane over the area to be covered. Use a blunt tool to press the cane into the groove. A wedge-shaped piece of hardwood works well (Illus. 45). Tap the wedge with a hammer. Work the cane into the groove gradually to avoid breaking it. When the cane is worked down into the groove on all four sides, spread a thin coat of glue in the groove on top of the cane, and then press the spline into the groove. Use a long block of soft wood to protect the spline as you gently

Illus. 45. Use a wedge of hardwood to drive the cane into the groove. The end of the wedge should be rounded so that you won't break the fibres.

hammer it into place (Illus. 46). When the spline is installed, use a sharp knife to trim away the excess cane around the outside edge (Illus. 47).

As the cane dries, it will tighten and smooth out. The cane can be left in its natural unfinished state, or you can spray it with clear polyurethane for added protection. If you want to darken the color of the cane, mask off the other areas of the door and spray lacquer stain on the cane.

Illus. 46. Use a piece of soft wood when you drive the spline into the groove. A long piece, such as the one here, helps to prevent dents in the spline.

Illus. 47. When the spline is in place, trim away the excess cane.

MOULDINGS

Another way to decorate doors and drawer fronts is to apply a moulding to the face (Illus. 48). The mouldings can be mitred to form square corners (Illus. 49), or you can use special curved-corner mouldings instead (Illus. 50).

If you don't plan on refinishing the entire door, prefinish the mouldings before you apply them. If you are applying the mouldings to bare wood, it's best to use aliphatic resin. However, this type of glue won't stick very well to a finished surface; so, when you are applying mouldings to finished surfaces, use panel adhesive instead.

Illus. 48. You can also decorate the front of a plywood door by applying a moulding to the surface.

Illus. 49. The moulding can be mitred to make a square corner.

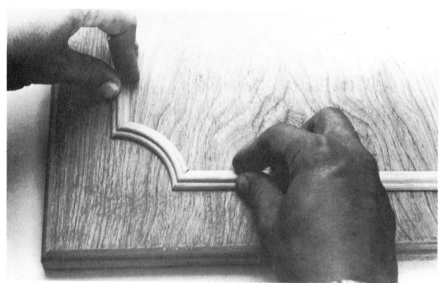

Illus. 50. A special curved piece of moulding is required to make this type of corner.

Cut a small hole in the caulking-tube nozzle so that the bead won't be too big. Apply the glue to the back of the moulding with a caulking gun. Run a small bead in the center of the moulding. Test for the correct amount by pressing a scrap against the bead. The bead should flatten out to cover most of the back of the moulding but not squeeze out past the edge. Draw a faint pencil line on the door front to indicate the position of the moulding. Place the moulding so that it just covers the line and hold it in place with tape (Illus. 51). You can also use a few small brads to hold the moulding in place. Drill pilot holes through the moulding to prevent splitting. Set the brads with a nail set and fill the holes with a putty stick.

Another type of moulding can be used to make a convincing imitation

Illus. 51. Masking tape can be used to hold the moulding in place until the glue dries.

of a panel door (Illus. 52). This moulding fits over the edge of the plywood. Since the moulding has a ⅜″ overhang, when it's used on a ¾″-thick door the result is a lipped door that will fit the standard ⅜″ lip hinge (Illus. 53). Lipped doors and overlay doors must be cut down before you apply the moulding. Flush doors, on the other hand, do not need to be trimmed; adding the moulding converts them into lipped doors.

You can use a commercially made moulding, such as the one shown in

Illus. 52. The moulding applied around the edges of these doors makes them resemble panel doors.

Illus. 53. This commercial moulding has a contoured face. Notice how the moulding lips over the edge of the door.

Illus. 53. This type is usually about 1½″ wide and available in several different shapes.

The moulding in Illus. 52 is wider than the commercial type; it's 2½″ wide, but you can make it any width you choose. To make the moulding, start with a ¾″-thick board. Cut the desired width, and then use the table saw to make a wide rabbet on the back of the board. The rabbet is ⅜″ deep. The width of the rabbet is ⅜″ less than the width of the board. This produces an L-shaped moulding. Now, mitre the corners of the moulding and apply it to the doors with panel adhesive and brads. When the glue has set, you can install the hinges. Use ⅜″ lipped hinges that attach to the rear of the door. Don't use any type of hinge that attaches to the moulding since it's not secured firmly enough to be used for hinge attachment.

3
Plastic Laminate

Covering the surface of old cabinets with plastic laminate can be a very effective way of improving the looks and serviceability of old cabinets, and plastic laminate is more durable and easier to clean than a painted surface (Illus. 54).

Plastic laminate comes in $\frac{1}{16}''$ and $\frac{1}{32}''$ thicknesses. The $\frac{1}{16}''$ thickness is the most readily available. Although you can use it for any application, the $\frac{1}{16}''$ thickness should always be used for counter tops and other areas that will receive a lot of wear. The $\frac{1}{32}''$ thickness can be used for vertical surfaces that won't receive as much wear, such as cabinet doors, drawer fronts, and face frames.

Doors made from $\frac{3}{4}''$ plywood, whether flush-lipped or overlay, particularly lend themselves to being covered with plastic laminate. If the edges of the door are rounded, you will need to cut them down to square edges. If the door is lipped, this may mean that to reuse the same door, you will have to change it to a flush door. Or you could trim off the lip and then glue a new strip of wood to the edge; by doing this, you can convert the door to a full overlay. Flush doors will usually need to be trimmed $\frac{1}{16}''$ smaller to allow for the self-edge of plastic laminate. If the doors have excessive clearance, then you don't need to trim them. Generally, overlay doors don't need any modification if the edges are square, unless there won't be enough clearance between the doors with the addition of the plastic laminate.

The plastic laminate is applied with contact cement. Contact cement will adhere to a previously finished surface if the surface is free from any grease and is not glossy. However, in most cases, you will need to thoroughly clean the doors with a grease-cutting cleaner and then remove the gloss by sanding. A belt sander makes the job easier. If the finish is in poor condition, sand to bare wood. Use nonflammable contact cement to avoid the possibility of an interaction with the finish;

Illus. 54. Plastic laminate applied to flat plywood doors can update the style of the cabinets and provide a much more durable and easy-to-clean surface.

flammable contact cement will lift some finishes, causing poor adhesion. Prepare both sides of the doors and all edges.

When you have prepared the doors, drawer fronts, and face frames, cut the plastic laminate to size. Cut about ½″ extra in both length and width to allow for trimming later on. *Wear eye protection when cutting plastic laminate.* The laminate is brittle and small sharp chips can fly into your face as you cut. You can use a table saw or a hand scoring knife. If you cut a large sheet on the table saw, you will need helpers to hold the unsupported side and back edges. You may want to use the scoring knife to cut the sheet into more manageable sizes. The scoring knife has a carbide cutter. Use a straightedge to guide the knife, and score the face side along the cutting line several times until the cut is about halfway through the laminate (Illus. 55). Apply pressure to one side of the line with the straightedge, and lift the other side until the laminate snaps apart at the score line.

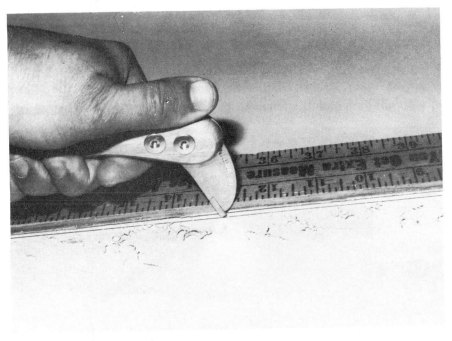

Illus. 55. The carbide scoring knife cuts plastic laminate in a manner that is similar to cutting glass. First you score a line with the knife; then you bend the laminate up until it breaks along the line. For best results, cut about halfway through the laminate with the knife.

With doors, you should apply the plastic laminate to both the front and the back. If you applied it only to the front, it could cause the door to warp. The laminate applied to the rear is called a balance sheet. It doesn't need to be the same pattern or color as the front sheet (only the same thickness) so that you can use a less expensive type of plastic laminate for the back if you want to. Since drawer fronts and face frames are small, they usually don't require a balance sheet.

Apply the balance sheet first. Coat the rear of the door and the back side of the laminate with contact cement. Using a small paint roller is a quick way to apply the cement (Illus. 56). When the contact cement is dry enough so that none of it transfers to your finger when you press against the surfaces, apply the laminate.

If the pieces are small, you can usually apply them without a slip sheet. Line up one edge, allowing a ¼″ overhang on all sides. Hold the laminate away from the surface of the door, except along one edge; then lower the opposite edge, slowly working the laminate down against the wood with your other hand.

When the doors are very large, it may be difficult to line the laminate up correctly. You only have one chance. Once the cement contacts, the

Illus. 56. Using a small paint roller makes it easy to get an even application of contact cement.

laminate is stuck, so you may need to use a slip sheet. This is another piece of plastic laminate that is a little larger than the one you are applying. This laminate must not have any contact cement on it. Place the slip sheet on the surface of the door, and then put the laminate that has been coated with contact cement on top of the slip sheet. Pull the slip sheet out a little so that about an inch of the door is exposed. Line up the laminate and press it against the exposed section of the door. Slowly withdraw the slip sheet and press the laminate into place.

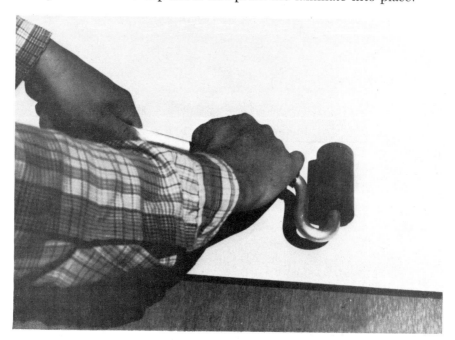

Illus. 57. With the J-roller, you can apply even pressure to the plastic laminate to improve the bonding.

For optimum adhesion, the laminate should be rolled down. For a project as large as kitchen remodelling, it's a good idea to invest in a J-roller, which is specifically designed for this job. Place the door flat on a solid work surface with the laminate facing up. Place the roller on the laminate and press down hard on the roller. Roll over the entire surface several times (Illus. 57). Be careful as you approach the edges; if you roll off the edge, you may break off the overhang.

A router with a laminate-trimming bit is the best tool to use for trimming the laminate flush with the edge. Clamp the door to a work-bench and trim off the excess laminate (Illus. 58). Although the router works faster, you can also use a scoring-edge trimmer, if you don't have a router (Illus. 59). A scoring-edge trimmer works the same way as a scoring knife, but it has a guide that rubs along the edge of the door to

Illus. 58. Using a router with a flush trimming bit is the fastest way to trim the laminate. The bit pilot rides against the side of the door to guide the router.

make the cut in line with the edge. After scoring, bend the excess laminate up until it snaps off (Illus. 60). Unless the job is very small, you probably will be better off using a router. The scoring-edge trimmer is useful for trimming tight corners and doing small jobs, but it's too slow for production work, such as covering a whole set of kitchen-cabinet doors.

Now, apply the self-edge to the edges. If you aren't applying a balance sheet, this would be the first step. Cement the top and bottom edges in place and trim them flush; then apply the sides. If you use a simple jig, like the one in Illus. 61, trimming the edges will be easier. This jig consists of one board clamped to the bench and another board nailed to the edge of the first board. Leave a small gap between the bottom edge of the vertical board and the bench; this will allow the excess laminate on the edge of the door to slip under the vertical board. With this setup, you can apply laminate to two edges at once before trimming. To use the

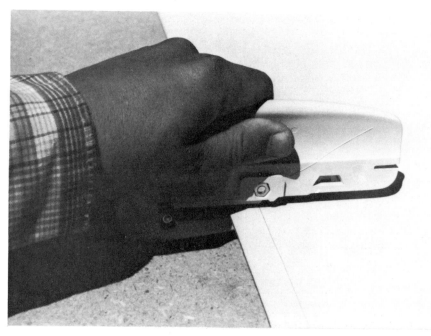

Illus. 59. A scoring-edge trimmer is slower than the router, but it can be useful on small jobs. It has a guide that rides along the door edge to guide the scoring knife.

jig, place the door against the vertical board and clamp it with a spring clamp. Rout off the excess from the edge on top, and then turn the door over and rout the second edge. Another way to trim the edges is to mount the router on a router table; this is particularly useful for small drawer fronts.

After you have trimmed the sides, apply the plastic laminate to the front of the door. The front is done last so that the exposed edges will be

Illus. 60 (left). After scoring the line, bend the laminate up, using the notch in the end of the trimmer. Illus. 61 (right). Trimming the edges will be easier if you use this simple jig.

on the sides. If you applied the self-edge last, there would be a small dark border around the front of the door from the exposed edge of the laminate. If you are using color-through laminates, this wouldn't be a problem. But it would still be a good idea to apply the front last because this way there would be less of a chance of marring the surface while you're trimming the edges. Apply the front sheet; then roll it down and trim it flush the same way you did the back sheet.

If the face frames will show with the doors closed, they should also be covered with plastic laminate. Cut the laminate into strips slightly wider than the stiles and rails (Illus. 62). You can either mitre the corners or use butt joints. After the laminate is in place, use a router to trim it flush with the edge of the face frame.

When the orientation of the pattern is unimportant, you can use the following method to cover the face frames. Cut a sheet of laminate that is large enough to cover an entire area of the cabinet—one section of drawers, for example. Apply cement to the entire rear surface of the sheet and to all of the face frames in the area to be covered. Place the full sheet over the area. Drill an entrance hole in each opening or use a router bit that drills its own entrance hole; then rout around each opening to trim away the excess laminate. This produces a cabinet face with no joints. It uses up more material than the other method, but it involves less cutting and joint fitting.

After you have installed all of the plastic laminate, remove any glue or marks from the surface with a mild detergent solution. Stubborn glue spots may require a special solvent, specifically designed for the type of glue you used.

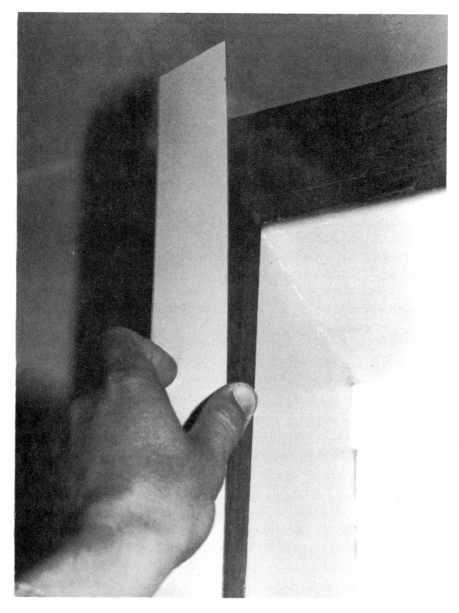

Illus. 62. Face frames can be covered with strips of plastic laminate that match the doors.

4

New Doors and Drawer Fronts

When the new style you want can't be achieved by modifying the existing doors and drawer fronts, you can still reuse the cabinet carcass and make new doors and drawer fronts (Illus. 63). This process is actually less disruptive than the other processes discussed in this book because the kitchen can be left intact while you build the new doors and drawer fronts and only needs to be disturbed long enough to remove the old ones and install the new ones.

When you build new doors, you can use a different type of hinge or make a completely different type of door. Don't limit yourself to the style of your original doors. Full overlay doors are easy to make and they completely cover the face frames, so you may want to consider using this type instead of lipped or flush doors (Illus. 64).

PLYWOOD OR PARTICLE-BOARD DOORS

Any of the door styles shown earlier that can be used for remodelling old doors can also be used when you are making new doors; simply start with a new piece of plywood or particle board instead of reusing an old door. Plywood and particle board are good materials to use for new doors when the style permits. Plywood is available in several hardwood face veneers. Particle board is available with a plastic-laminate face in either a solid color or an imitation wood-grain pattern.

There are three basic types of cabinet doors: flush, overlay, and lipped (Illus. 65). A flush door fits inside the face frame, and the front of the door is flush with the face frame. The flush door must fit the opening accurately or it won't look good. Measure the opening and then make the door ⅛" smaller. This will allow for a ¹⁄₁₆" gap around the door. Bevel the edges of the door 2° towards the rear of the door so that the door will open without the rear corner hitting the face frame. If you are using butt hinges, cut gains in the edge of the door for the hinges to be mounted in.

Flush doors are difficult to fit; so, even if the original doors were flush, you may want to switch to an overlay door or lipped door when remodelling. Since these doors hide the opening when closed, their fit isn't as critical.

Overlay doors are larger than the opening. The entire thickness of the door is outside of the face frame (Illus. 66). This is the simplest type of door to make; it is just a rectangle with square edges. Special hinges are required for overlay doors, so you will need to change the hinges if you are switching from another type of door.

Lipped doors are probably the type most commonly used in older carpenter-built cabinets. They hide the opening as do overlay doors, but

Illus. 63. New doors applied to old cabinets can completely change their style.

only half the thickness overlaps the face frame. A rabbet cut around the edge of the door makes the lip (Illus. 67). The edges were usually rounded on older lipped doors, which gives them a somewhat dated appearance. You can leave the edges square to make the new doors look more modern. Lipped doors require special hinges that have an offset bent into the leaf.

To make a lipped door, cut the door ¾″ larger than the opening. Set the dado blade on a table saw to make a ⅜″-wide rabbet ⅜″ deep. Place the door with the back against the table and an edge against the fence, and cut a rabbet on all four sides. When two lipped doors meet without a

Illus. 64. Since full overlay doors completely cover the face frames, you can change to a new style without further modifications to the cabinet.

mullion, they are not lipped on the edge that meets. Many cabinets don't have a bottom face-frame rail on the base cabinets. In such cases, the bottom edge of the door is not lipped.

Edge Treatments   When the edges of a plywood or particle-board door are visible, it is usually desirable to cover them. The two most common materials to use are veneer tape and plastic T moulding.

Veneer tape is a thin wood veneer bonded to a paper backing. It is applied to the edge of the door or drawer front with contact cement or a heat-sensitive backing. The tape comes in $^{13}/_{16}''$ and 2″ widths and in rolls that are 8' long or longer. The tape is available in several popular wood species, so you can match the face veneer or you can use it as an accent on a door with a plastic-laminate-covered face (Illus. 68).

To apply the tape, cut a strip a little longer than the edge to be covered and apply contact cement to the back of the tape and the door edge. When the cement is dry, place the tape on the edge, allowing an overhang on all sides (Illus. 69). Trim off the excess tape from the ends with scissors and use a sharp knife to trim the sides (Illus. 70). Use a

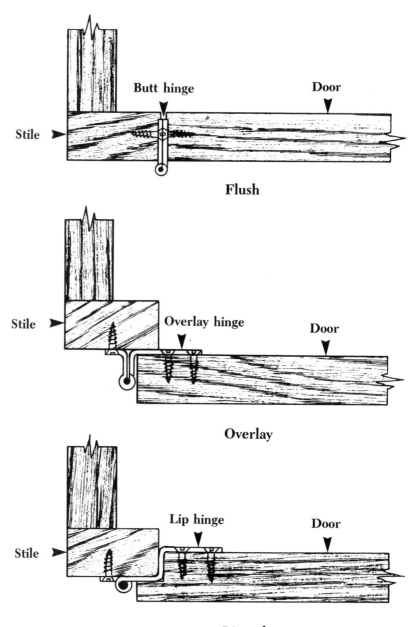

Flush

Overlay

Lipped

Illus. 65. Three basic types of cabinet doors.

Illus. 66. Overlay doors fit over the face frame. You can make the doors large enough to completely cover the face frames, or you can leave some of the face frame showing, as seen here.

Illus. 67. Lipped doors have a rabbet around the edge. Half of the door's thickness lips over the face frame.

Illus. 68. Veneer tape is used to hide the edges of plywood or particle board. In this case, it is applied to the edge of a particle-board door that has plastic laminate on the face.

Illus. 69. Apply the veneer tape so that there is an overhang on all sides.

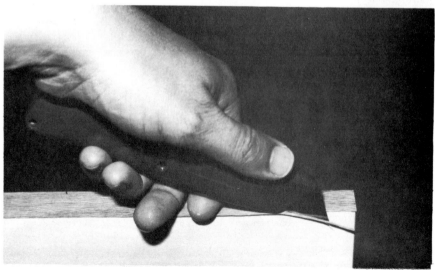

Illus. 70. After applying the tape, trim the excess off with a sharp knife.

small wallpaper-seam roller to roll down the tape; then sand the edges flush, using 150-grit sandpaper and a sanding block.

Some veneer tape is available with a heat-sensitive adhesive backing, so no contact cement is needed. Just put the tape in place and iron it down with a hot clothes iron.

Plastic T moulding is often used when the doors are made from plastic-laminate-covered particle board. The moulding has a barbed tail that fits into a slot in the edge of the door (Illus. 71 and 72). The slot can be

 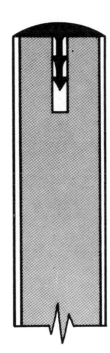

Illus. 71 (left). Plastic T moulding has a barbed tail that fits into a kerf in the edge of the board. Illus. 72 (right). This diagram shows how the barbed tail of the plastic T moulding fits into the kerf.

cut on the table saw, but you need to use a blade that makes a thinner kerf than usual. A special router bit can also be used to make the slot. The moulding will bend around corners if a V-shaped notch is cut out of the tail at the point of bending. The corners of the door should be slightly rounded with a file. It's best to use a single piece of moulding all around the door. Place the joint in the middle of the most inconspicuous edge. Cut notches at the corners to allow the moulding to bend. Use a rubber mallet to drive the tail into the slot. Leave the moulding a little bit long and then trim it to length at the joint where the two ends meet.

PANEL DOORS

Panel doors are a traditional favorite, and now that special sets of router bits are available it's easier for the home craftsman to make them (Illus.

73). Each panel door consists of a frame—made from two side stiles, a top rail, and a bottom rail—and a center panel (Illus. 74).

The center panel can be made from ¼″ plywood (Illus. 75) or from a thicker piece of solid wood. When the thicker piece of solid wood is used, the edges are bevelled so that the panel will fit into a ¼″ groove in the frame. When this process is done, it is called a raised panel (Illus. 76).

Wood expands and contracts with changes in humidity. The panel door is designed to eliminate problems caused by these changes. The frame will remain relatively dimensionally stable because wood doesn't

Illus. 73. Panel doors can give cabinets a country or traditional look.

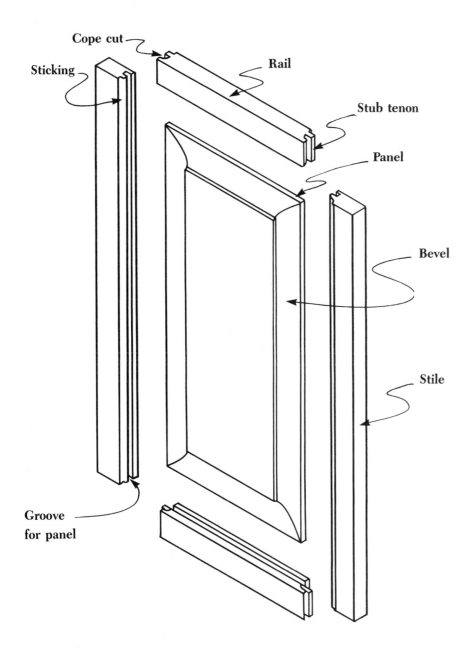

Cope cut

Rail

Sticking

Stub tenon

Panel

Bevel

Stile

Groove
for panel

Illus. 74. Parts of a panel door.

change appreciably along the long-grain length. Most movement occurs across the width, and the wider the board, the greater the change will be. The panel floats inside the frame; it is not glued in place, and the groove where it fits is deep enough to allow for expansion. However, when plywood is used for the panel, it can be glued in place because plywood doesn't expand and contract the way solid lumber does. If a solid lumber panel is glued in place, it may eventually split or force the frame joints open.

The width of the frame members depends a lot on personal taste. In most kitchen doors, they are 1½″ to 2″ wide. When an arched top is

Illus. 75. These doors have a flat plywood panel.

used, the top rail must be wider, usually 3½″ to 4″. In most cases, the bottom rail is the same width as the stiles, but it can be made wider, depending on the look you want. The inside edge of the frame is frequently decorated with a moulded edge called sticking; when this is done, the joints must be shaped to fit over the sticking. These joints are called coped joints.

The frame members and the panel can be made on a table saw or with a shaper or a router. The table saw is especially useful for making simple doors without arched tops or decorative sticking. The shaper or router can be used to produce the fancier, arched top doors with decorative sticking and coped joints. Since the shaper is an expensive piece of equipment, most home craftsmen do not have access to one. The router, on the other hand, is a common piece of home shop equipment, so making panel doors with a router will be covered here in detail. (The operation is similar on the shaper.) Then there will be a similar discussion on making panel doors on a table saw.

Using the Router   There are several types of bits you can use with a router to make raised panel doors. The exact procedure for using the bits varies from manufacturer to manufacturer, so follow the directions that come with your bits. The procedure described here is representative of most types, but some details will vary from one set to another. The operation is much easier if you mount the router in a router table.

Rip the stiles and rails to width on a table saw; then cut the stiles and rails to the exact length required. The length of the stiles should be equal to the finished height of the door. The length of the rails can be calculated by subtracting the combined width of both stiles from the overall width of the door and then adding twice the depth of the groove in the stile. For example, if you need a 12″ overall finished width for a door and the stiles are 1½″ wide, multiply 1½″ by 2 to get 3″ and then

Illus. 76. Solid lumber is used to make a raised panel.

subtract 3″ from 12″ to get 9″. If the groove in the stiles is ⅜″ deep, add 2 times ⅜″, which equals ¾″, to 9″ to get the length of 9¾″ for the rails.

Now, set up the router to make the coped joints on the ends of the rails. This is done first because cutting on end grain tends to produce a chipped-out section where the bit exists; by cutting the ends first, any chipped-out area will be removed as the edges are moulded. Set the bit as shown in "A" of Illus. 77; the shoulder at the top should be equal to the shoulder on the sticking that you will cut later. Even though the bit has a pilot to guide it, you will have more control when you're making straight cuts if you also use the router table fences. Set the fence so that the edge of the work will lightly touch the bit pilot. Use an L-shaped piece of plywood as a support block as you cut the end joints (Illus. 78). Clamp the rail to the support. This will keep the rail from twisting out of alignment because the tail of the support will ride against the fence. Use a piece of scrap to check the setup before cutting the first joint. The rail should be placed with its face side up when you are making this cut. Initially, you should perform all of the steps for one door and then test-

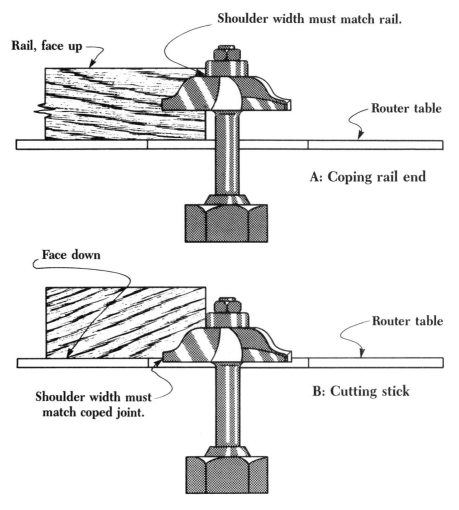

Illus. 77. A: Setup for coping rail ends. B: Setup for cutting stick.

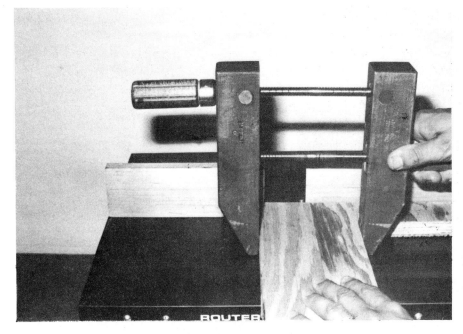

Illus. 78. Clamp the rail to a support block when you are cutting the end joints.

assemble it. After you are confident that the setups are correct, cut all of the joints in the project at the same time so that you will only need to set up the router once for each operation.

Next, install the slotting bit, and set it up to cut the tenon as shown in "A" of Illus. 79. This cut is also made with the face side of the rail up. The tenon thickness should be equal to the thickness of the slotting bit; this same bit is used to make the groove where the tenon will fit. When all of the tenons have been made, reinstall the moulding bit and set it up to cut the sticking. Adjust the depth until the shoulder left by the bit is equal to the shoulder on the coped joint (see "B" of Illus. 77). Cut the sticking on both the stiles and the rails with the face side down against the router table.

The final operation to be performed on the stiles and rails is cutting the groove. Reinstall the slotting cutter. To properly position the groove, place one of the rails face up on the router table and adjust the router depth of cut until the slotter is in line with the tenon on the end of the rail (see "B" of Illus. 79).

When you are making a very narrow door, the rails may end up too short to be handled safely. When this happens, vary the procedure just described by first cutting the sticking and groove in a longer piece; then cut it to length and make the stub-tenon joints. Be sure to clamp the rail to a support block so that it will be easier to handle and you will be able to keep your fingers away from the bit.

Since the router bits have a pilot to guide them, they will follow a curved edge. This makes it easy to build doors with arched tops. Cut the arch in the top rail before routing and the cutter will automatically follow

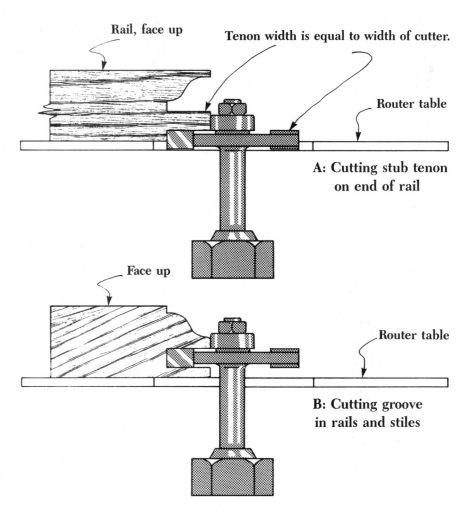

Rail, face up

Tenon width is equal to width of cutter.

Router table

**A: Cutting stub tenon
on end of rail**

Face up

Router table

**B: Cutting groove
in rails and stiles**

*Illus. 79. A: Setup for cut-
ting the tenon. B: Setup for
cutting the groove.*

the curve. You will need to remove the fence from the router table to
perform this operation (Illus. 80 and 81).

The joint formed by the routing operations is a stub-tenon joint (Illus.
82). This joint will have adequate strength for moderately used doors,
but as you can see in Illus. 27 in Chapter 1, heavy use can cause the joint
to break. For added strength, use blind dowels in the joints when you
are assembling the frames (Illus. 83). Use a dowelling jig to align the
holes in the tenon and the groove in the stiles. Use ¼″ dowels. They will
be the same width as the tenon. As you can see in Illus. 83, this means
that the sides of the holes will break through the sides of the tenon. This
isn't a problem; just make sure that you use long enough dowels so that
they extend past the tenon into the rail.

You can use either flat panels or raised panels with a frame prepared
according to the instructions just discussed. To determine the width of a
flat plywood panel, subtract the combined width of the stiles from the
finished size of the door and then add two times the depth of the groove.
The height is determined in a similar manner; but if the top rail has an

arch cut in it, be sure to use the thinnest dimension of the top rail in the calculations.

An interesting variation on the flat panel is the cane-covered panel (Illus. 84). (Refer to Chapter 2 for details about sheet cane.) First cut the plywood panel, and then cut a piece of cane slightly larger than the panel. Don't soak the cane as is usually done; apply it dry. The cane is attached with a special adhesive that comes in a spray can. It's available at crafts shops and from some mail-order woodworking suppliers. Spray the back of the cane with this glue. Don't apply any glue to the panel. Press the cane onto the panel. It will stick without any clamping. Trim the cane to the size of the panel, and then the panel can be installed in the frame. You may need to make the groove in the frame slightly wider than normal. The door shown in Illus. 84 was finished after the cane had

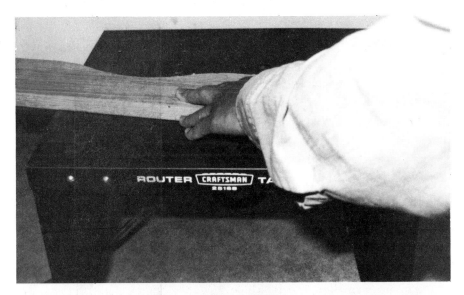

Illus. 80. The fence must be removed from the router table when you are routing the arched top. The pilot on the router bit will guide the cut.

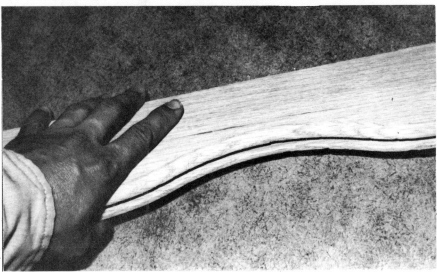

Illus. 81. After you have routed the arched top, you can see that the bit has followed the contour of the top exactly.

Illus. 82. The completed stub-tenon joint, ready to be assembled.

been installed, and the cane received the same finish as the rest of the door. If you would like the cane to contrast with the door finish, apply the finish to the plywood panel before attaching the cane; then after you have assembled the door, mask off the panel area while you apply the finish to the rest of the door.

Since raised panels are made from solid lumber, you need to take into account dimensional change. Determine the size of a raised panel the same way as described for plywood panels, and then subtract ⅛″ from both the height and the width; this will allow for a ¹⁄₁₆″ clearance on all four sides of the panel. The panel is not glued into the groove; it is free to expand and contract inside the frame. Large panels will need to be glued up from smaller boards. Make sure the edges are true and square,

Illus. 83. Dowels added to the joint will increase the strength of a stub tenon.

Illus. 84. You can cover a flat plywood panel with cane.

and then apply woodworking glue to both mating surfaces. Assemble the panel using bar clamps. Keep the panel flat by using at least three clamps. Place two of the clamps on the lower face near the ends and one clamp in the middle on the upper face. If you have more clamps, use them; alternate between the upper and lower positions.

If you want ½″-thick panels, the easiest method is buying ½″-thick lumber. If you have access to a thickness planer, you can also plane down ¾″-thick panels to ½″ after you've glued them up. Or, you can resaw ¾″-thick lumber to ½″; do this before gluing up the panels. Rip the individual pieces into a size that your saw can handle; then glue up the panel after resawing.

You can use the method described on page 71 to cut the bevels on a table saw, or you can use a special router bit to raise the panels (Illus. 85). With the router, you have the advantage of being able to make arched top panels (Illus. 86). The router also leaves a much smoother cut, so less sanding is needed. Usually the panels are made from ½"-

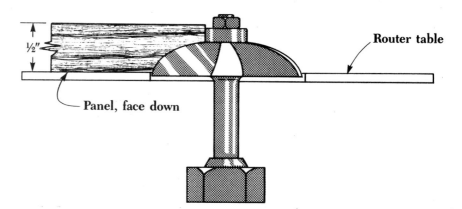

Illus. 85. A panel-raising bit.

thick lumber and bevelled on one side only, but you can use ¾"-thick lumber if you bevel both the front and the back, as shown in Illus. 87. For straight edges, use the fence on the router table. The arched top must be cut without the fence using the bit pilot to guide the work. Make the cut with the face side of the panel against the router table. Rout the end grain first and then rout the edges. This will remove any tear-outs left from routing the end grain.

When you are assembling the door, apply glue only to the frame joints; don't allow any glue to get into the groove for the panel. You can, however, put a small daub of silicone rubber glue in the groove in the

Illus. 86. The pilot on the router bit will follow the contour of the arched top panel.

middle of the top and bottom rails. This will keep the panel in alignment and yet still allow it to expand and contract. Make sure that all surfaces of the stub-tenon and coped joint receive an even coat of glue. A small stiff brush, such as the type used for applying soldering flux, is useful for spreading the glue.

Place a bar clamp across the rails to clamp the joints. If the door tends to twist or cup as the clamps are tightened, clamp it down to the bench with C-clamps or hand screws.

After the glue has dried, use a sharp chisel to scrape any squeezed-out glue from the joints. The stiles and rails may vary slightly in thickness; this will be noticeable where they meet at the joint. You can smooth out the joint with a cabinet scraper or an orbital sander. A belt sander won't work because the grain changes direction at the joint, but an orbital sander isn't affected by grain direction.

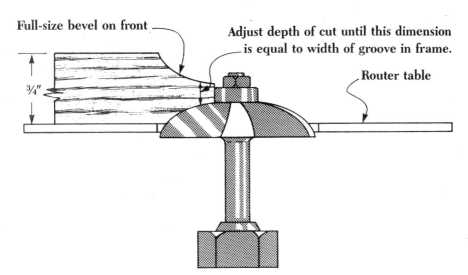

Illus. 87. Bevelling both the front and back of the panels allows you to use ¾"-thick lumber.

Using the Table Saw When you make panel doors on the table saw, the frame will have square edges instead of the moulded ones produced by the router, but other than that the results are similar. *Some of the operations that follow will have to be performed with the guards removed, so be sure to use caution and keep your hands clear of the blade.*

Rip the frame members to width and then cut them to length; the length of the stiles should be the same as the finished height of the door. The length of the rails will depend on the type of joint you choose. You can make stub tenons on the table saw, but you can also make haunched tenons or spline joints. Spline joints are the easiest to make, and they are the type that will be described here (Illus. 88). For a spline joint, the size of the rails is determined by subtracting the combined width of the stiles from the finished width of the door.

Set the table-saw dado blade to make a ¼"-wide × ½"-deep cut, and

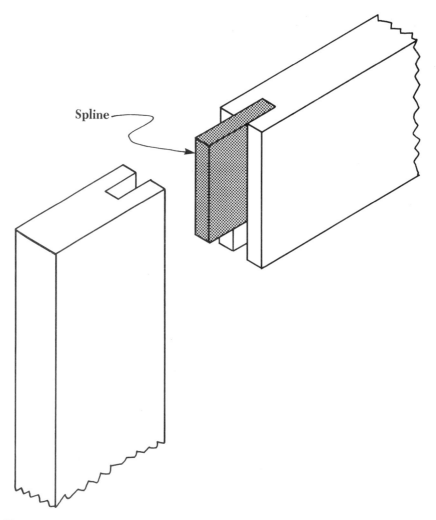

Spline

Illus. 88. A spline joint has about the same strength as a stub-tenon, but it is easier to make with a table saw.

make a groove in the inside edge of the frame members. The groove should be centered in the edge so that there is ¼″ on either side of the ¼″-wide groove.

To make the spline joint, cut a groove in each end of the rails using the same dado-blade setup. Clamp the rails to an L-shaped support block, such as the one used with the router in Illus. 78. The support block will keep the rail from tipping and help to keep your fingers away from the blade. If you have a tenoning attachment for the table saw, use it to hold the rail as you cut the groove for the spline; it will make the job easier and safer.

The splines are made from ¼″ tempered hardboard. Use the type that is smooth on both faces. Cut a strip 1″ wide and then cut it into the individual splines. The length of the spline is equal to the width of the rail minus ½″.

The panel is made from ½″-thick lumber; it should be ¾″ larger in both dimensions than the inside opening of the frame. This allows for ⅜″ inside the groove and a ⅛″ clearance.

Mount a smooth-cutting saw blade on the table saw and set it to make a ⅛″-deep cut. Set the rip fence for 2″. Now, make the shoulder cuts on the face of the panel.

Mount a 10″-wide plywood auxiliary fence to the rip fence of the saw. This will help steady the panel as the bevels are cut. Make a zero-clearance table-saw insert by cutting a piece of plywood or hardboard to fit in the blade-insert opening; then lower the blade below the table and install the insert. With the tilt arbor set to the correct bevel angle, turn on the saw and slowly crank up the blade until it cuts through the insert. The zero-clearance insert will keep the edge of the panel from slipping down into the blade opening in the standard insert. Raise the blade to a cutting depth of 2″, and then adjust the tilt arbor to make the bevel. Most saws don't have markings that are accurate enough to rely on when you are setting this angle. So it's best to place the panel against the fence with the shoulder cuts facing out; then adjust the angle until the teeth touch the bottom of the shoulder cut and the panel is ¼″ thick at a point ⅜″ in from the edge (Illus. 89). Make a test cut on some scrap to check the setup before cutting the actual panel. Make the cuts across the top and bottom first, and then bevel the sides. Sand off the saw marks before assembling the door.

Apply glue to the splines and the grooves where they fit, but don't put any glue in the groove for the panel. As explained before, the panel must float freely in the groove.

Assemble the door as shown in the exploded view (Illus. 90). Clamp the door with bar clamps and use a framing square to make sure it is square.

If you want to use this type of door in a lipped-door application, cut the lip after you have assembled the door.

The door shown in Illus. 91 uses the same type of frame and spline joints, but the middle panel is made from plywood. The V-pattern of grooves in the panel is made by assembling two half-panels with diagonal grooves.

The panels will look best if the grain also runs diagonally. To make it do so, begin with two pieces of plywood that are large enough to be cut into several half-panels. Cut grooves running with the grain in the large pieces of plywood. You can use the table saw or a router to make the grooves. To cut the pieces of plywood into the small half-panels so that the grain and the grooves run diagonally, make a 45° cut on one corner of the sheet using a mitre gauge. In order to be able to arrange the panels in a V-pattern, make the 45° cut on the right corner of one sheet and on the left corner of the other. Next, set the fence for the width of the half-

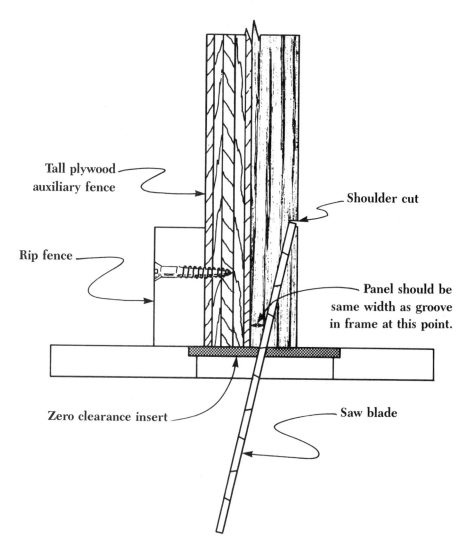

Tall plywood auxiliary fence

Shoulder cut

Rip fence

Panel should be same width as groove in frame at this point.

Zero clearance insert

Saw blade

Illus. 89. Cutting the panel bevel on the table saw.

panel and place the plywood with the 45° edge against the fence. Cut the plywood into as many strips as needed; then use the mitre gauge to cut the ends square and cut the panels to length. Adjust the cuts so that the grooves line up in a V. A simple way to do this is to cut the parts a little bit long and then align the grooves as you glue the panel together. When the glue is dry, trim the panel to the correct size. Before gluing the panel together, bevel the edges with the table-saw tilt arbor set to 45°. This will produce the V-groove down the middle and around the edges of the panel.

Use the same dado-blade setup that you used for cutting the grooves in the frame to cut a groove in all four sides of the panel and on the two edges of the half-panels that meet in the center. Cut 1″-wide splines from tempered hardboard, and place a spline in the joint when you glue the two halves of the panel together. Assemble the door as shown in the exploded view (Illus. 92). The splines on the edges extend the full length of the stile. The splines in the rails are 1″ shorter than the rail. Since the panel is made of plywood, you can glue it in place.

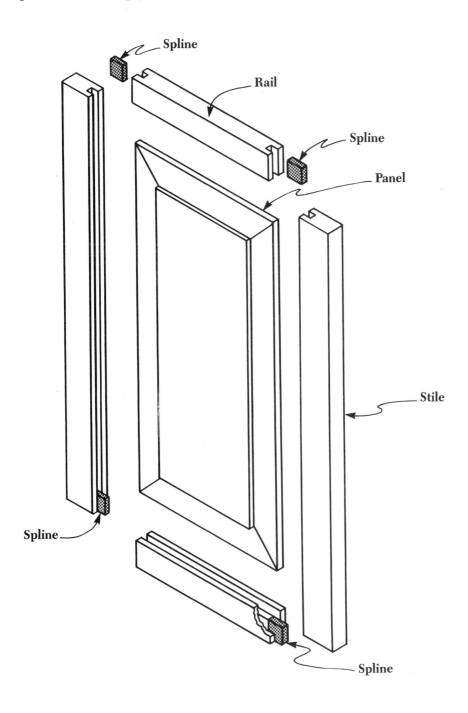

Illus. 90. Panel door, exploded view.

Illus. 91. The frame for these doors is made with the table saw. The panels are made from two pieces of plywood that have been grooved and assembled in a V pattern.

GLAZED DOORS

A door with a pane of glass in it can be an attractive accent in a kitchen-cabinet installation. Clear glass can be used for a display area (Illus. 93), and an etched- or stained-glass panel can add decoration (Illus. 94–96).

If you are using glazed doors in a project in which you are also using panel doors, make the frames for the glazed doors the same way as you make the frames for the panel doors. Assemble the frames without a panel, and then use a router with a rabbeting bit to make a rabbet on the inside of the door for the glass. This method will still allow the stub tenons or splines to fit into a groove at the joints. The rest of the groove is cut away by the rabbeting bit, leaving a rabbet for the glass.

If you don't need to match the construction of other doors, you can make a simple frame for a glazed door, as shown in Illus. 97. The frame members should be 1½" to 2" wide and joined at the corners with blind dowel joints. After you have assembled the frame, use a router to cut a rabbet around the inside edge of the opening. Make the rabbet ⅜" deep and ¼" wide. The frame can be lipped after assembly for a lipped-door application or used as a flush or overlay door.

Clear glass or plastic is held in place with a ¼" × ¼" strip of wood called a stop. The stop is nailed in place with small brads, or you can use a plastic stop that staples in place. The glass should be cut ⅛" smaller than the opening. Stained-glass panels have a lead channel around the

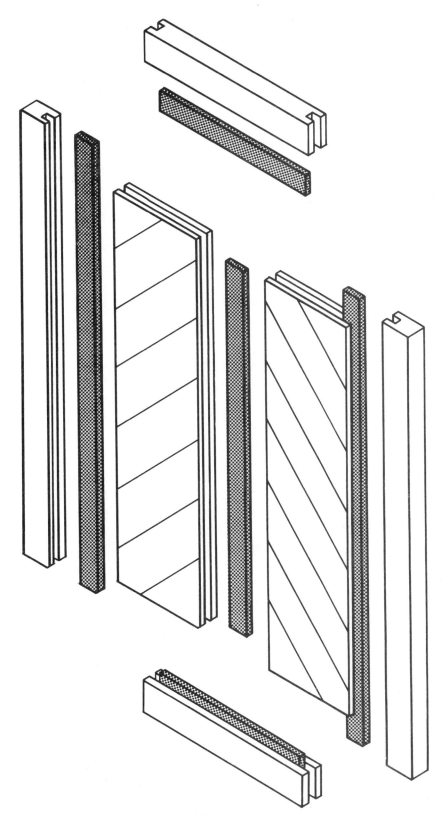

Illus. 92. V-groove panel door, exploded view.

Illus. 93 (left). Clear glass in place of the wood panels can make an attractive display cabinet. Illus. 94 (right). Clear glass with an etched design adds some decoration, while still allowing the contents of the cabinet to show.

Illus. 95 (left). Frosted glass allows the shape of the objects in the cabinet to show, while hiding some of the clutter. Illus. 96 (right). Stained glass is decorative, and provides an accent point in a group of cabinets. The glass is set in lead channels.

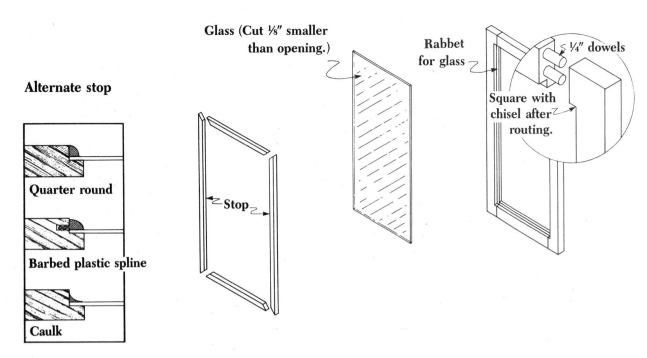

Alternate stop

Quarter round

Barbed plastic spline

Caulk

Glass (Cut ⅛″ smaller than opening.)

Stop

Rabbet for glass

¼″ dowels

Square with chisel after routing.

Illus. 97. Glazed door, exploded view.

edge. This will fill up most of the rabbet, so there will be no room for a stop. Instead, use small brass turn buttons attached to the rear of the door to hold the glass in the rabbet. The turn buttons allow you to remove the glass for replacement or cleaning. If you prefer, the glass can be held in place with a bead of silicone caulk. The caulk is available in colors that match the wood finish, or you can use silver-colored caulk to match the lead channel.

DRAWER FRONTS

The new drawer fronts should harmonize with the new doors, but they don't need to be identical. Since the drawer fronts are smaller, certain types of decoration won't fit on them; and in terms of panel construction, there may not be enough room for a panel unless you decrease the width of the stiles and rails. Frequently, the drawer fronts are simply made from a matching piece of wood with no decoration.

When overlay drawer fronts are used in conjunction with panel doors, the drawer fronts can be bevelled the same way as the panels, but no frame is necessary.

If the old drawer fronts are easily removable, then it is best to remove them when replacing the fronts (Illus. 98). However, when the fronts are an integral part of the drawer, as is often the case, removing them can be difficult. If the drawer fronts are the flush type, the new fronts can be installed on top of them and the drawer will become an overlay type. If the drawer is already an overlay type or it's lipped, cut the front down to the same size as the drawer opening in the carcass. Usually there is enough extra room at the back of the cabinet to allow the drawer to go in flush; then you can apply the new fronts over the old ones.

Attach the new fronts with screws driven from the rear through the old fronts. You may need to get longer screws for the handles if the ones supplied won't reach through both fronts. You can install the handles before attaching the fronts, but using longer screws for the handles will give added strength to the front joint. This way there will be less of a chance of the front pulling off.

Illus. 98. If the drawers already have false fronts, it is easy to remove them and replace them with new fronts.

FACE FRAMES AND END PANELS

If you make the new doors from a different species of wood from that of the originals, you will need to cover the other exposed portions of the cabinets with matching wood. The exposed ends can be covered with ¼" plywood. Cut the plywood to fit the shape of the end and then attach it with panel adhesive. If you choose to use full overlay doors, the face frames will be completely hidden when the doors are closed, so you may not need to do anything to them. When the face frames show, you can cover them with 2"-wide veneer tape (Illus. 99). Thoroughly clean the face frames to remove any grease, and sand off the gloss from the finish. Apply the tape with contact cement, following the directions on pages 53–57.

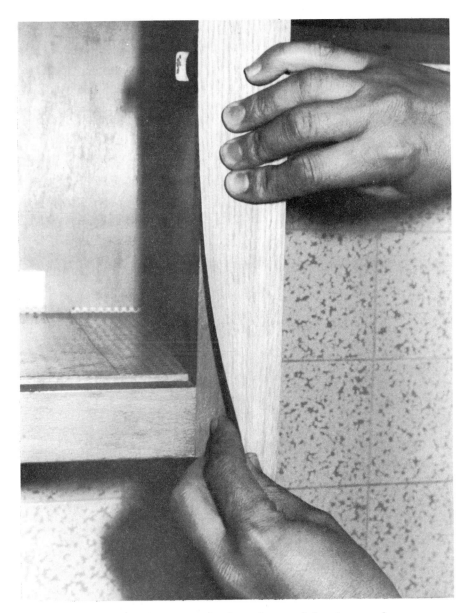

Illus. 99. When a different species of wood is used for the new doors, cover the face frames with 2″-wide veneer tape to match.

5
New Hardware

New hardware may be all that's needed to give old cabinets a new look (Illus. 100), and usually you will also want to install new hardware when you make new doors and drawer fronts. There are three basic types of cabinet hardware: pulls, hinges, and catches.

Illus. 100. Sometimes all that's needed to change the look of your cabinets is some new hardware.

PULLS

Pulls come in a wide range of styles. Most pulls are mounted with two machine screws in the rear. Pulls with exposed screws on the front are sometimes used on rustic or country-style cabinets.

Pull placement is largely a matter of personal preference. Generally the pull is placed on doors near the edge opposite the hinge, and in the lower corner of overhead cabinet doors and the upper corner of base cabinet doors. When space permits, try to keep the pulls about 1½" in from the edge and 2" from the top or bottom. On panel doors, it may be better to center the pull on the stile, even though this will usually be less than 1½" in from the edge. For the sake of style, the pulls are sometimes centered in the middle of the door, but this isn't very convenient for day-to-day use.

Illus. 101 shows a simple guide that is used for marking the hole locations for pulls. You can make a guide from a piece of hardboard and a scrap of wood. Start with a piece of wood about ¾" thick, 1½" wide, and 4" to 6" long. Make a groove in the middle of one edge; the groove should

Illus. 101. A placement guide like this one makes it easy to locate the holes for a pull.

be ¼" wide and ⅜" deep. Next, glue a piece of ¼"-thick tempered hardboard into the groove. Lay out the location of the pull holes on the hardboard and drill holes that are the size needed for the pull screws. To use the guide, rest the wood block against the edge of the door and position the guide the correct distance from the top or bottom edge. Drill through the holes in the guide and through the door.

Drawer pulls are usually centered on smaller drawers and placed near the top of larger ones. You can use a guide similar to the one made for the door pulls if all of the drawers will be the same. But usually the drawers are of several sizes; so, to center the pull, you must measure each one individually.

A continuous wood pull strip can add style to plain, painted, or laminate-covered doors (Illus. 102). The pull is available in several wood

Illus. 102. This continuous oak pull gives the cabinets a sleek contemporary look.

species, and can be purchased from a local moulding dealer or from some of the mail-order woodworkers' suppliers. Finishing the pull will be easier if you do it before installation. You can finish it in long strips, and then you can apply finish to the cut ends after cutting the strips to length. Don't finish the tongue area of the pull; the glue will adhere better if this area is left unfinished (Illus. 103).

When you are installing this type of pull on old doors, the doors must be cut down in size. Mark the location of the cut; then place masking tape over the cut line on both sides of the door. This will help prevent splintering as the door is cut. Set the table-saw fence for the correct distance and cut off the bottom edge of overhead doors and the top edge of base cabinet doors.

The rest of the procedure for installing the pull is the same for both new and old doors. Put a dado blade on the saw and set it to the

Illus. 103. It is easier to finish the pull while the moulding is still in long lengths. Don't apply any finish to the tongue area; it needs to be left unfinished for the glue to adhere properly.

Illus. 104. You can use a dado blade on the table saw to cut the groove for the pull. Use a tall auxiliary fence to help steady the door.

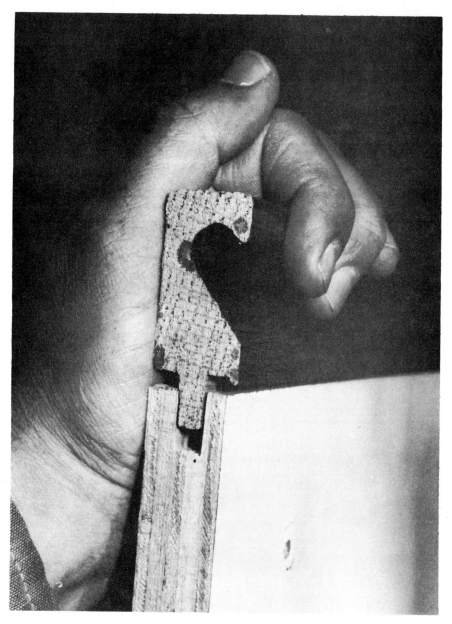

Illus. 105. The tongue on the pull should fit snugly into the groove, but not too tightly or it will force all of the glue out of the joint.

thickness of the tongue on the pull. Use a tall plywood auxiliary fence to help steady the door and cut a groove along the edge of the door (Illus. 104). The pull fits into the groove, as shown in Illus. 105. When this type of pull is used with a plastic-laminate-covered door, you can conceal the joint on the edge of the door by applying the plastic laminate to the edge after the groove has been cut. Cut off 1/16″ from the end of the tongue and fit it into the groove, as shown in Illus. 106.

Glue the pull to the door edge and clamp it with bar clamps (Illus.

Illus. 106. When the door edge is covered with plastic laminate, you can hide the tongue on the pull.

Illus. 107. Use bar clamps to hold the pull in place while the glue dries. Note that the pull is protected with a piece of scrap wood and that one clamp is placed on the front face to keep the pull from twisting. Don't tighten the clamps too much or you may break the pull.

107). Unless you have several clamps, this operation will be a bottleneck that will slow down production when you have a lot of doors to do. If you don't mind the delay, simply leave the door in the clamps until the glue has set. To speed up the process, you can secure the pull with nails and then remove the clamps. With the clamps in place, drill three small pilot holes through the back of the door into the tongue of the pull, one in the middle and one about 2″ in from each edge. Drill the holes at a slight angle so that you can use ¾″ brads without breaking through the face of the door. Place a piece of tape on the drill to mark the depth. Drive ¾″ brads into the holes. They will now hold the pull as the glue sets, so you can remove the clamps and proceed with the next door.

This type of pull can also be applied to drawer fronts. It's easiest if the fronts are removable; but if the drawer front extends above the drawer sides enough, you can cut it down and make the groove with the front still attached to the drawer.

HINGES

The type of hinge you choose depends on the design of the door and the cabinet carcass. You can use simple butt hinges on flush doors, but most other types will require hinges specifically designed for them.

Regardless of the type of hinge you use, the following tips on installation should be helpful. You will probably be installing quite a few hinges; this can be tedious if you install the screws by hand. Therefore, an electric screwdriver or a variable speed drill with a screwdriver attachment would be a good investment if you don't already have one (Illus. 108). The screws will be easier to drive and there will be less of a chance

Illus. 108. With an electric screwdriver, you can remove and install many hinges much easier and faster.

of the wood splitting if you drill pilot holes first. In soft wood, you can push an awl into the wood instead of drilling a pilot hole. Self-closing hinges tend to shift position slightly as the screws are tightened, which can lead to the door binding on the edge opposite the hinge. To avoid this, allow a little extra clearance as you install the hinge; when you tighten the screws, the hinge will spring over and bring the clearance to the normal amount.

When you are installing new hinges on an old face frame, change the position slightly so that you don't reuse the old holes. You can usually still hide the old holes with the new hinge if you position it carefully.

For Lipped Doors   With lipped doors, you need to use a hinge that has a bent leaf to fit the rabbet in the edge of the door (Illus. 109). This type

Illus. 109. A hinge with an offset bent into the leaf is used with lipped doors. Note the routed gain for this hinge. This reduces the gap between the door and the face frame. Usually the hinge leaf is thin enough so that no gain is needed.

of hinge attaches to the rear of the door and the front of the face frame. This makes installation easy because you can see how the doors line up before you attach them to the face frame. First attach the hinges to the door, and then put the door in place and line it up with the adjacent doors. When the position is correct, attach the hinges to the face frame, using one screw per hinge. Now, test the door to make sure it opens freely. If it does, put in the second screw. If the door binds, loosen the screws and adjust the position; then put a screw in the second hole and tighten it, but leave the first screws loose. If the door opens freely now, tighten the first screws. If the amount of adjustment wasn't too great, the hinge should stay in place as you tighten the screw and the door will still open freely; if the hinge changes position as you tighten the screw, remove the screw and make a new hole for it in the proper position. You may need to angle the screw hole slightly away from the old one to keep the screw from wandering back into the old hole.

For Overlay Doors You can install overlay doors with hinges that are attached to the front of the face frame, or you can use fully concealed hinges instead. The first type is very similar to the hinges described for lipped doors. The straight leaf is attached to the rear of the door (Illus. 110); then the door is placed on the cabinet and the hinge is attached to the face frame (Illus. 111).

 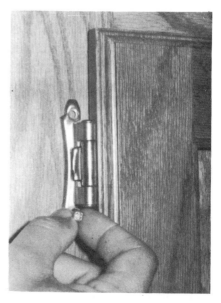

Illus. 110 (left). This type of overlay-door hinge is similar to the lipped hinge except that the leaf is straight. The leaf is attached to the back of the door. Illus. 111 (right). Both this type of overlay hinge and the lipped hinge are attached to the face frame after they have been attached to the door. This makes it easy to position the door correctly.

The fully concealed type comes in several varieties. Follow the manufacturer's directions because dimensions can be critical. One popular type of concealed hinge requires a 35-mm hole to be drilled partway through the rear of the door. A cup on the hinge fits into the hole. The hinge comes in two parts: one is mounted on the door, the other on the cabinet; then when both parts are installed, the hinge on the door is slipped onto the mounting plate on the cabinet and the set screws are tightened to hold it in place (Illus. 112). Since this type of hinge is adjustable, you can line up the doors and adjust the clearances after you've installed the hinges. This is particularly useful when you are installing new doors on old carcasses; if the carcass is out of square, you can adjust the hinge to compensate. These hinges were first designed for use on cabinets without face frames. However, most older cabinets have face frames, so you will need to make special accommodations. You can get a special mounting plate to attach the hinge to a face frame, or you can add a block of wood behind the face frame to which you can attach the hinge. When you have a lot of hinges to install, a guide, such as the one described for door pulls, will speed up the process. Use the guide to drill pilot holes for the mounting plates in the side of the cabinet and to position the 35-mm hole in the door.

Semiconcealed hinges have all of the mounting screws hidden, but a small hinge pin is visible from the front (Illus. 113). This type can be

Illus. 112 (left). This type of overlay-door hinge is adjustable and fully concealed. The mounting plate is attached to the cabinet before the door is installed; then the hinge on the door is attached to the plate with a set screw. Illus. 113 (right). A semiconcealed type of overlay-door hinge has a small exposed pin, but the rest of the hinge and the screws are concealed.

mounted so that it overlaps the top and bottom of the door, but you'll get a more professional installation if you make a notch in the door for the hinge (Illus. 114). The notch can be in the top and bottom edge of the door, as shown in Illus. 114, or it can be spaced in from the edge as

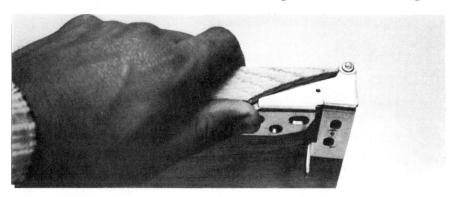

Illus. 114. The hinge fits into a diagonal notch in the edge of the door.

shown in Illus. 115. Use a table saw to make the notch. Lower the blade so that it is just a little higher than the thickness of the door (Illus. 116). If the notch is in the edge, install a plywood auxiliary fence on the rip fence of the table saw to prevent the blade from hitting the metal fence. Use the fence to guide the door for both placements. Test the setup on scrap until you are satisfied with the result. Advance the scrap into the saw until the blade cuts a notch in the outer face that is large enough for the protruding pin of the hinge. Test-fit the hinge in the slot. You may need to raise or lower the blade to get the correct length and angle on the slot. If you can't get the correct angle, try using a blade with a different diameter. When the setup is correct, cut the slots in the doors. You will need to reposition the fence on the other side of the blade to make the second notch in the door, so cut the first notch in all of the doors at the same time and then move the fence to the other side and cut all of the second notches.

Illus. 115. The notch can be placed in from the edge, as shown here, or on the edge, as shown in Illus. 114.

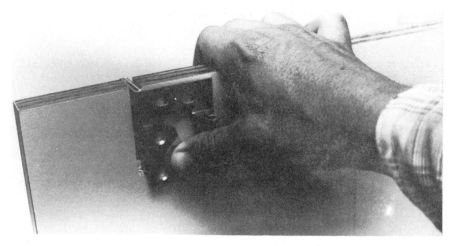

Illus. 116. You can use a table saw to cut the diagonal notch. A large-diameter blade usually works best. Note that this photo has been taken from the fence side of the blade with the fence removed. Normally you couldn't see this view because the fence would be in the way. Use a wood auxiliary fence to prevent the blade from touching the metal fence.

CATCHES

If you don't use self-closing hinges, you will need to install catches on the new doors. There are two basic types of catches: magnetic and friction. Magnetic catches are popular because they don't need to be adjusted as accurately as friction catches. However, both types require an initial adjustment and both are installed in a similar manner.

If possible, it's best to place the catch near the middle of the edge of the door opposite the hinges. This placement will hold the door closed better should it warp slightly. If there is a central mullion or a permanently attached shelf near the middle, this would be an ideal location for attaching the catch. Place the catch on the side of the mullion or the underside of the shelf. If there isn't a mullion or shelf available, then attach the catch to the top or bottom rail of the face frame. Some catches require a greater mounting area than the area that is available on the edge of a face frame; in these cases, you may need to attach a block of wood to the rear of the frame. When you can't install the catch in the middle of the edge, the next best location would be at the top. The worst location would be at the bottom of the door since the catch would be on top of the bottom shelf and would be in the way.

When mounting the catch, place the screws in the middle of the slotted holes to allow adjustment in both directions. Put the catch on the cabinet first. Attach the latch plate to the catch in its proper position and then firmly close the door. The latch plate has one or more spikes that will mark the location on the door (Illus. 117). If it doesn't mark, adjust

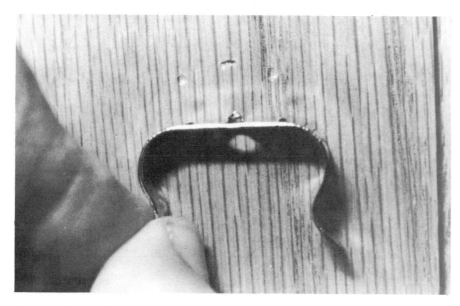

Illus. 117. Spikes on the catch latch plate will help locate the plate on the door. Notice the marks left in the wood by the plate.

the catch out farther; then attach the latch plate to the door in the indicated position and see how it works. You may still need to adjust the catch in or out to get the door to close tightly.

6
Shelves

If all of the shelves in your cabinets are permanently fixed in one position, the chances are that you have at least a box of cereal lying on its side in one of your cabinets. Fixed shelves just don't accommodate all the sizes of the things that need to be stored in kitchen cabinets. Either you waste a lot of space with shelves that are too far apart, or the shelves are too close together and tall items won't fit. The answer is adjustable shelving. If you are building a new cabinet, install adjustable shelving so that there will be at least one cabinet that will accommodate all of the odd-size requirements. If you are remodelling an old cabinet, you may want to consider replacing some of the fixed shelves with adjustable shelves.

Fixed shelves are usually attached to the carcass with cleats or dado joints. Shelves attached with cleats are easy to convert to adjustable shelves (Illus. 118). Simply remove the screws from the cleat or pry it off if it is attached with nails. The shelf can be reused with any of the shelf supports described later. A shelf attached with a dado joint is more difficult to convert to an adjustable shelf, but it can be done. Cut the shelf as close to one side of the cabinet as you can with a sabre saw; then bend the shelf down and out of its dado. Cut a strip of wood to fill in the dado, and glue it in place. Since the shelf will be too short to reuse, you will need to make a new one unless you use a handsaw instead of the sabre saw and cut the shelf very close to the side of the cabinet. You will more than likely run into several nails when cutting this close to the side, so it is probably best to make a new shelf.

Two types of adjustable shelves are popular for use in kitchen cabinets. One type involves metal standards and clips to support the shelf (Illus. 119). When building new cabinets, it is customary to install the standards in grooves cut with a dado blade. When working with existing

Illus. 118. This shelf would be easy to remove and make adjustable because it is attached with cleats that are secured with screws.

cabinets, you can surface-mount the standards (Illus. 120). The standards are attached with screws or special nails that are supplied with them. Each slot in the standard is numbered. Install all four standards so that they are touching the bottom of the cabinet and the same numbered slot

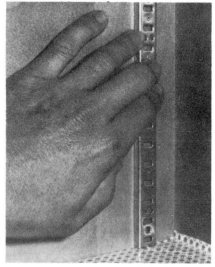

Illus. 119 (left). These metal standards are placed in grooves in the side of the cabinet. The clips can be moved to any of the slots, providing a wide range of shelf positions. Illus. 120 (right). When remodelling, the standards may be surface-mounted.

is at the bottom. This way all of the slots will line up and you can use the numbers to install the clips. If you have to cut the standards to length, cut them at the top, leaving the factory end at the bottom. Cut the shelves to fit between the standards and install the clips in the desired locations; then place the shelves on top of the clips.

The other type of adjustable shelf is very well suited for remodelling work because you don't need to add a standard. It involves a clip with a pin that fits into a hole drilled in the side of the cabinet (Illus. 121). Since no standards are used, it is possible to fit the shelves tightly between the sides of the cabinet without getting the gap that is left when surface-mounted standards are used. You don't need to drill a lot of holes; you can lay out the positions of the shelves and just drill three holes about 1" apart. This will give you 3" of adjustment if you want to change the shelf position (Illus. 122). When you want full adjustability, drill a series of

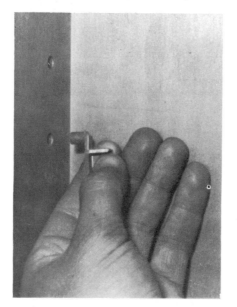

Illus. 121 (left). This shelf support fits into a hole drilled in the side of the cabinet. The holes are easy to add to an existing cabinet. Illus. 122 (right). Three holes at each location are often all that's needed for adequate adjustment. This shelf is at the center hole location, so it can be adjusted 1" higher or lower.

holes in the sides (Illus. 123). A piece of pegboard makes a good guide. Just place the pegboard against the bottom of the cabinet and drill through the holes. Wrap a piece of tape around the drill bit to indicate the hole depth so that you won't drill through the other side. The same method of drilling holes can be carried out with a similar type of shelf support that is used for glass display shelves. The type of clip that's used is the only difference (Illus. 124).

When you are installing new shelves made from plywood or particle board, cover the front edge with a facing strip. You can use veneer tape or plastic T moulding (refer to pages 53–57) or you can make a facing strip from a piece of solid lumber.

Illus. 123 (left). A full set of holes gives the maximum adjustability. Illus. 124 (right). With glass display shelves, you can use a similar type of support that also fits in holes in the sides of the cabinet.

7

Drawers

You can add a drawer to an existing cabinet or incorporate it in a new cabinet. Drawer construction in fine cabinets can be very complex, often involving sophisticated joints and guides, but most kitchen cabinets only require the simple drawer construction shown in Illus. 125.

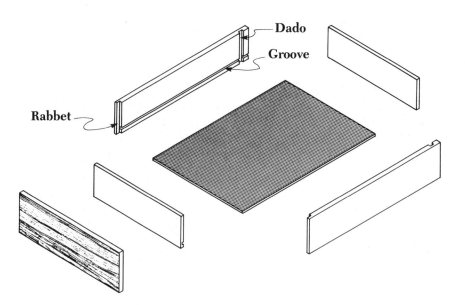

Illus. 125. Simple drawer, exploded view.

    The drawer in the example that follows is easy to build and sturdy. It's made from ½"-thick material, but ¾"-thick stock can also be used. Begin by ripping the sides and front to width, and then cut a ¼" × ¼" groove ½" up from the bottom edge using a dado blade on the table saw (Illus. 126). Next, make a ½"-wide by ¼"-deep dado ½" in from the back of the sides, using the table-saw setup shown in Illus. 127. Illus. 128 shows the completed dado. Use a similar setup to cut a ½"-wide by ¼"-deep rabbet on the front edge of the sides (Illus. 129). Notice that both of these cuts

Illus. 126. After ripping the sides to width, make a groove in the sides for the bottom.

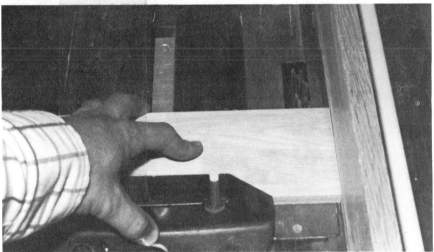

Illus. 127. To make the dado for the back of the drawer, set the dado blade to the thickness of the back and set the fence so that the dado is ½" in from the back of the side.

Illus. 128. The completed dado for the drawer back.

must be made on the correct ends of the sides. Hold the sides together with the grooves facing each other, and mark the front and back ends before making these cuts.

Cut the back from ½"-thick stock. Its width should be ¾" less than the width of the sides.

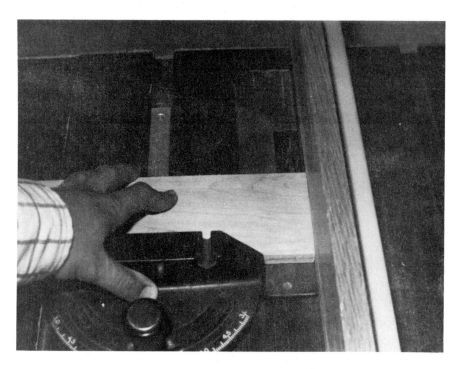

Illus. 129. The drawer front fits into a rabbet in the side. Make the rabbet using the dado blade. The wood auxiliary fence keeps the blade from hitting the metal fence.

Assemble the drawer using glue and nails or screws. The back should be placed so that the bottom is flush with the top edge of the groove in the side (Illus. 130).

Install the bottom. The bottom is made from ¼"-thick hardboard or plywood. It should be a snug fit in the grooves. Slide it in from the rear, and before nailing, use a framing square to make sure that the drawer is square. After squaring up the drawer, nail the bottom to the back with box nails spaced 2" apart (Illus. 131).

Make the false front to match the rest of the drawers if you're only adding a new drawer. If you are replacing the door and drawer fronts with new ones, you can choose a new style for the false front. When you are using panel doors, you can simply use a flat drawer front with a shaped edge as shown in Illus. 132, or you can make panel drawer fronts. If the drawers are small, you may need to decrease the width of the stiles or rails to leave room for the panel (Illus. 133).

Attach the false front to the front of the drawer with screws driven from the rear (Illus. 134).

Unless you have experience in building drawers, you will probably find that it is easier and the drawer will work better if you use a commercial drawer guide. The center-guide type is the easiest to install and doesn't require any side supports. With this type of guide, the drawer is made slightly smaller than the opening. Center guides are available in several styles. One style involves a metal guide and plastic rollers (Illus. 135). Another involves a wood center rail that has a T-shaped cross section and a plastic guide that attaches to the rear of the drawer (Illus. 136). Side guides (Illus. 137) are a little harder to install and you need to make the drawer smaller to allow for the guides on the sides, but they are much stronger and will probably last longer than center guides.

To install a new drawer in an existing cabinet, you will need to cut out an opening for it. Use a sabre saw. It may be necessary to drill an

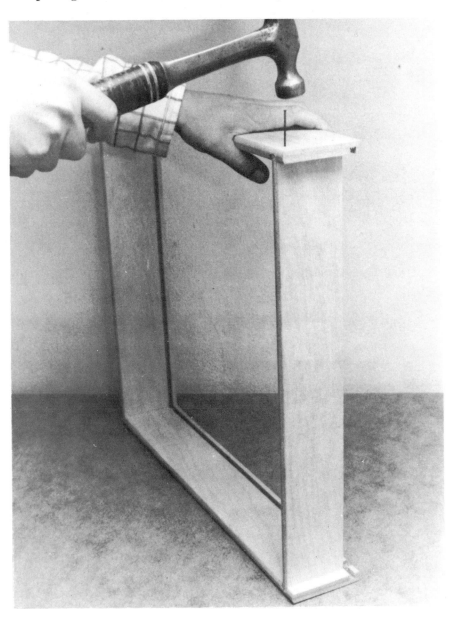

Illus. 130. Assemble the drawer using glue and nails or screws.

Illus. 131. Make sure that the drawer is square; then nail the bottom to the back of the drawer.

Illus. 132. Here, a simple, flat drawer front is used with panel doors.

Illus. 133. If you made the rails full width on this small drawer, they would completely fill the drawer front.

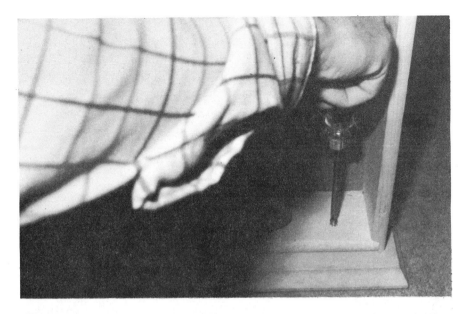

Illus. 134. The false front is attached to the drawer with screws driven through the front of the drawer and into the back of the false front.

Illus. 135. This style has a metal center guide attached to the face frame and the back of the cabinet. A plastic roller attaches to the back of the drawer, and rollers on the face frame guide the drawer sides.

Illus. 136. This style has a T-shaped wood center rail and a plastic guide attached to the rear of the drawer. In this photo, the drawer is upside down on the workbench and the center rail is in the plastic guide for a test fit.

entrance hole inside the waste area to insert the saw blade. Side guides don't require a rail below the drawer, but there must be a flat surface on both sides of the drawer where you can mount the guides. If the drawer will fit between two bulkheads, side guides will work well. The center guide must have a rail in the face frame below the drawer, but there doesn't need to be any support on the sides. So, if the drawer is in an area away from the ends or bulkheads, use a center guide.

Illus. 137. With side guides, there's a metal guide on both sides of the drawer and both sides of the opening. Side guides are the strongest and most trouble-free type of guide, but they are also the most expensive. When you're using side guides, the drawer must be smaller than the opening to allow room for the guides between the drawer sides and the sides of the cabinet.

8
Structural Changes

When your remodelling goes beyond the cosmetic effects of updating the doors and drawer fronts, you will need to do some demolition and rebuilding on the cabinet carcass. The space requirements of new appliances or your desire to correct deficiencies in the original layout of the kitchen may necessitate structural changes. If you are careful, you can reuse much of the material that is removed in the demolition process.

Three useful tools for demolition are the chisel, pry bar, and hammer. A wide chisel is useful for breaking glue joints and making an opening for the pry bar (Illus. 138). Since you may hit a nail in the process, don't

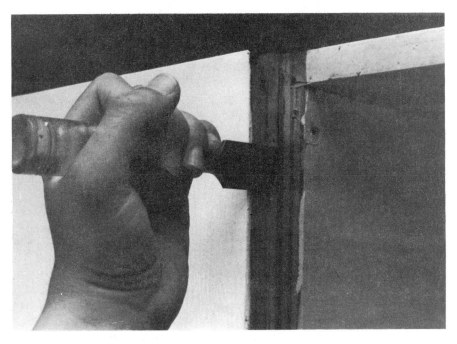

Illus. 138. Driving a chisel into a joint will open it enough to get the pry bar in.

use your best chisels for this purpose. Drive the chisel into the joint with a hammer until the gap is wide enough for the pry bar. A wide, flat pry bar works well for this type of demolition (Illus. 139). Because it is thinner than a regular pry bar, you can fit it into the joints easier and the wide blade is less likely to dent the surface of the wood. Keep repositioning the pry bar along the joint so that you will open the joint evenly and avoid breaking the board. You can also use a hammer to break open joints. Place a piece of scrap wood against the side below a dado joint, as

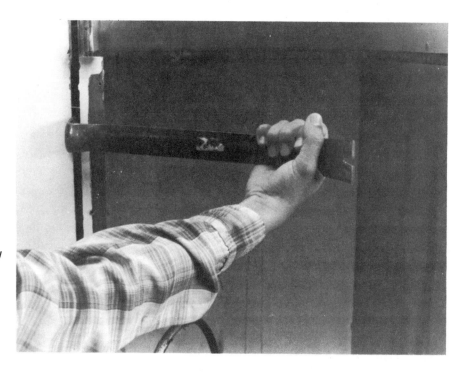

Illus. 139. Reposition the pry bar frequently to keep from splitting the board. Using the pry bar as shown, with the short claw in the joint, will often provide more leverage.

shown in Illus. 140. Hammer along the joint, using the scrap to protect the face of the wood. Move back and forth along the joint as you hammer so that the joint opens up evenly. If the wood around the joint begins to split, hold the scrap board over the splitting area.

Saws, screwdrivers, and other tools are also used extensively in disassembling cabinets. A nail set, for instance, can make it easier to remove a board without damage. If the board is attached with finishing nails, set the nails deeper with the nail set; this will make it easier to pry the board off. However, the nail set tapers, which will result in an enlarged hole and may even split the board if you set the nail too deep. A pin punch is a type of metal working punch that is similar to a nail set, but it has a long untapered end. If you use a pin punch to set the nails, you can drive them completely through the board. When a board is nailed to two other boards with nails that are 90° to each other, no matter how you pry it off, one of the boards will split; but if you drive one set of nails through the board with a punch or nail set, you can pry the board off with little or no damage.

Plan your remodelling carefully before starting on the demolition. Try to leave as much of the original cabinet in place as you can.

If the cabinets are factory-built, they are assembled from modules that are connected with screws. Find the screws in the face frame, the sides of the cabinets, and the back where it attaches to the wall, and then remove them. The cabinet is now free and can be pulled out. You can leave the modules intact and reposition them to change the layout.

Custom-built cabinets are usually built as a unit; to remove a section, cut through the face frames at the point where you will begin removing material. Place the chisel on the joint between the face frame and the carcass near one end of the board. Drive the chisel into the joint until there is a big enough gap for the flat bar. Then use the bar to pry the face frame from the carcass. Don't pry one end all the way off at once or you will break the board; instead, work along the full length of the board several times. If you plan on reusing the face-frame material, place the board face down on a work surface with the first nail slightly past the

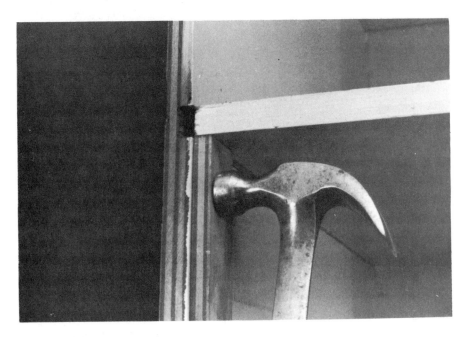

Illus. 140. Use a scrap of wood to protect the boards when you hammer a joint apart.

edge. Pound the nail through until the point is flush with the rear of the board; then slide the board until the next nail is past the edge and pound it through. When all of the nails are flush with the rear of the board, turn the board over and use a claw hammer to pull out the nails. Use a piece of plywood between the hammer and the face of the board to bring the surface closer to the head of the nail, making it easier to pry the nail out and protecting the face of the board.

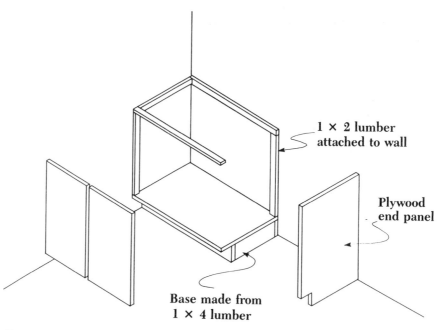

1 × 2 lumber attached to wall

Plywood end panel

Base made from 1 × 4 lumber

Illus. 141. This type of skeleton-frame construction is often found in older cabinets. Because it relies on the walls for strength, it is more difficult to relocate. You may need to disassemble the cabinet and rebuild it in the new location.

If the area to be demolished is at the end of the cabinet, the next step would be to remove the end panel. Protect the panel with a block of wood and use a heavy hammer to pound along the top joint. When the joint begins to open, move to the next joint down where a shelf attaches and pound it open; then move down until the bottom joint is loose. Now return to the top joint and pound it off, and then work down to the bottom joint.

With the end panel off, you can pry out the shelves. The top and bottom will usually be one continuous piece. Mark the location of the cut and use a sabre saw to cut them. The bottom of base cabinets is difficult to cut flush with an adjacent divider because the saw will hit the divider. In this case, use a handsaw. You may hit a few nails, so don't use your best saw for this procedure. Start with the teeth flat against the board and saw, applying downward pressure to the tip. As you start to get a kerf, angle the saw more and more until you break through the board; then cut normally along the line. Saw down through the toe kick and the base of the cabinet and then remove the shelves.

You can reuse the end panels and shelf materials if needed for boxing off the end of the cutoff cabinet or for building a cabinet in a new location.

Kitchen cabinets can be made by several types of construction, but the types usually fall into two basic categories: skeleton-frame construction and case construction. With skeleton-frame construction, the basic skeleton of the cabinet and shelves is made from small boards and the sides are attached to the skeleton. Kitchen cabinets usually employ a modified form of skeleton-frame construction, whereby the ends and the bulkheads are made of ¾″ plywood or particle board and a skeleton frame is used where the cabinets attach to the walls (Illus. 141). With case construction, ¾″ plywood or particle board is used throughout and rabbet and dado joints are used where the parts join (Illus. 142).

When you are cutting down the size of a cabinet or modifying it in some way, it's best to follow the same construction method originally used. However, when you must build a completely new section, case construction is usually the best method.

If the existing cabinets have face frames, try to match them as closely as possible. Face frames are usually ¾″ thick and 1½″ wide; but if the face frames in the existing cabinets have different dimensions, use the same dimensions they have. To get a very strong face frame, you should assemble the joints with dowels before installing the frame. However, many carpenter-built cabinets simply have the face-frame members

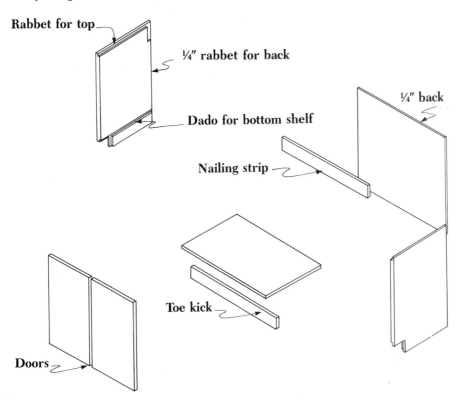

Rabbet for top

¼″ rabbet for back

¼″ back

Dado for bottom shelf

Nailing strip

Toe kick

Doors

Illus. 142. Case construction is used in most newer cabinets, but particularly in factory-built modular cabinets. Since the cabinet relies on its own structure for strength, you can easily relocate it after removing the screws that hold it in place.

glued and nailed with finishing nails. When this is the case, set the nails below the surface and fill the holes with putty.

Whether you are repositioning an old cabinet or installing a new one, you will need to attach it firmly to the wall. Cabinets should be attached directly to the wall studs. Hollow wall fasteners are not strong enough to withstand the combined weight of cabinets and their contents. An electronic stud finder will allow you to accurately find the wall studs. If you don't have an electronic stud finder, you can use a nail and tape measure to find the studs. If you have removed an old cabinet, find a nail hole in the wall that was used for attaching the old cabinet. Measure from this hole to the new location and make a mark at the nearest multiple of 16″ that falls inside the area where the cabinet will be mounted. Drive a nail

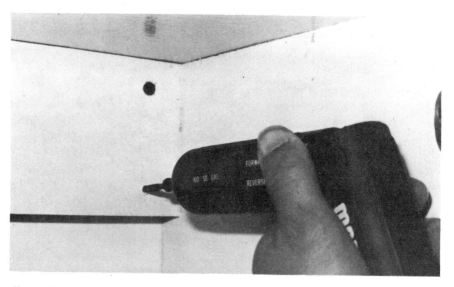

Illus. 143. To attach the cabinet to the wall, drive screws through the nailing strip into a wall stud. If the nailing strip is wide enough, use two or three screws at each stud location.

in line with this mark in an area that will later be hidden by the cabinet. If the studs are laid out accurately, you should hit one. If you don't hit a stud with the nail, then move the nail ½″ to one side of the mark and try again. If you still miss the stud, try ½″ away on the other side of the mark. Keep up this pattern until you find the stud. Once you have found the first one, measure 16″ away from it to find the next one and then drive a nail until you find the stud. If you don't have a nail hole to start from, use a corner of an electric switch or outlet as your starting point. Electrical boxes are usually mounted on a stud, but you don't know which side of the box the stud is on.

The cabinets should have a nailing strip along the top edge inside the cabinet. This is a piece of wood 1½″ to 3″ wide that is attached firmly to the sides and top of the cabinet. If the old cabinets don't have nailing strips, add them to make it easier to reinstall the cabinets. Nails can be used to attach the cabinets, but 3″ dry-wall screws are much stronger. Mark the stud locations on the nailing strip before placing the cabinet. Use clamps to hold the cabinet in position while you attach it to the wall. Screw through the nailing strip into the stud. If the strip is wide enough, put two or three screws into each stud; this is particularly important on overhead cabinets since the screws must carry the entire weight of the cabinet and its contents (Illus. 143). At the bottom of the cabinet, put screws through the back into the stud to hold the cabinet firmly against the wall. You can install a nailing strip at the bottom of the cabinet, but it is usually omitted since the top one carries the weight. On base cabinets, screw through the nailing strip at the top into the studs; then toenail a few nails through the toe kick into the floor to keep the cabinets from shifting.

9
A Typical Remodelling Project

You can see how all of the processes in the previous chapters fit together by following a typical kitchen-cabinet-remodelling project from start to finish. In this case, the existing cabinets are about 30 years old (Illus. 144). They are basically in good condition and made from quality materials, but time has taken its toll on the hardware. Most of the hinges need to be replaced and the drawer guides are worn. The original light-

Illus. 144. These 30-year-old cabinets are worth remodelling because they are built from ¾" birch plywood and are still basically in good condition.

birch finish wore out years ago and several coats of paint have since been applied. The original appliances need to be replaced. The existing layout with the separate oven and the cooking top leaves only a small work space on the counter.

The remodelling plan calls for some structural changes so that the cabinet will accommodate a drop-in range and provide more work space on the counter. The doors and drawer fronts and any other exposed surfaces will be covered with plastic laminate, and all of the present hardware will be replaced.

The first step is removing the doors (Illus. 145). You can use a power screwdriver to speed up the process (Illus. 146). These doors will be

Illus. 145. Begin the re-modelling by removing the doors. Since the doors will be reused, number them according to position.

reused. Since the doors are made from ¾″ birch plywood, they will provide a good smooth substrate for plastic laminate. Be sure to number the doors to keep track of their locations.

Remove the oven and cooking top next (Illus. 147), but remember to disconnect the plug before you work on them. If they are permanently-wired in, you may need to have an electrician disconnect them. When this is the case, have a range outlet installed at the same time so that you can simply plug in the new range.

Begin the required demolition using the methods discussed in Chapter 8 (Illus. 148). In this case, the section around the built-in oven needs to be removed. The materials will be salvaged to make a new overhead cabinet and a small base cabinet next to the new range. The base cabinet

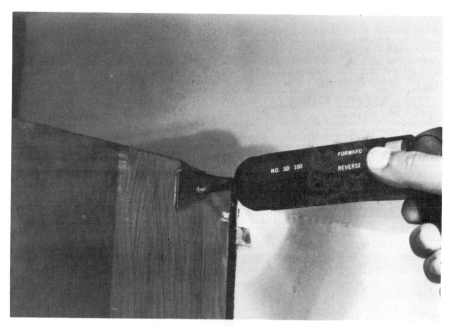

Illus. 146. Using a power screwdriver to remove the hinges speeds up the process.

below the cooking top will be reused but in a different location, so it needs to be removed (Illus. 149).

Begin building the new cabinets by cutting the salvaged pieces of the old cabinets into usable sizes. You can cut the large pieces into more manageable sizes with a portable circular saw. Place masking tape on the cutting line to prevent tear-outs along the cut (Illus. 150). When the pieces have been cut to length, use a table saw to rip them to width (Illus. 151).

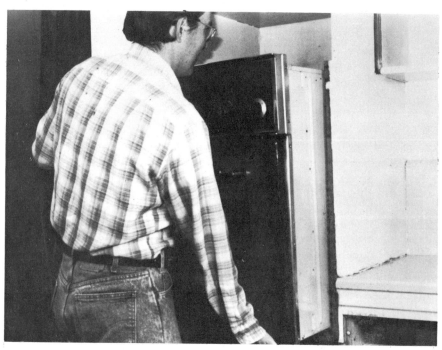

Illus. 147. Since this remodelling involves installing a new range, the next step is removing the old oven and cooking top. Be sure to turn off the circuit breaker, remove the fuse, or unplug the units before you begin to work on them.

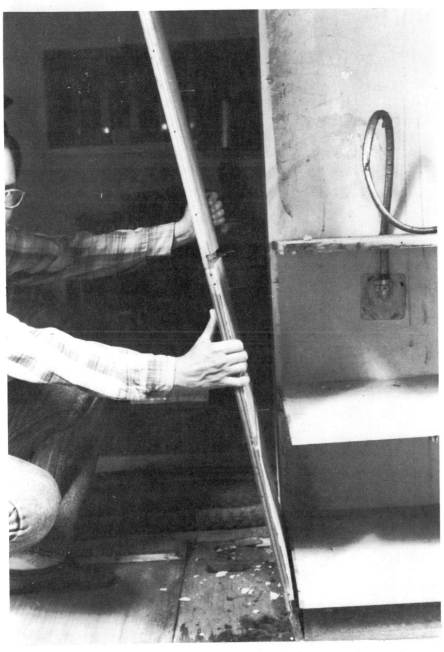

Illus. 148. Begin demolition by taking off the end panel of the cabinet to be removed.

To join the sides to the top and bottom, cut a rabbet in the side (Illus. 152). The rabbets should be ¾″ wide and ⅜″ deep. If you use a dado blade on the table saw to make the rabbets as shown in Illus. 152, then you should attach an auxiliary fence made from wood to the saw's rip fence to prevent the dado blade from touching the metal fence. Also, make a ¼″-wide by ⅜″-deep rabbet for the back. Make sure that you cut this rabbet along the back edge; since there is a right-hand side and a left-hand side, if you don't pay attention to this, you may end up with two right sides and no left side. This cabinet also incorporates a fixed

Illus. 149. The base cabinet below the cooking top is removed so that the base cabinet area can be rearranged to accommodate the new range.

Illus. 150. The end panel from the cabinet around the built-in oven provides lots of material you can reuse to make new cabinets. A portable circular saw can be used to cut the panel into smaller lengths. Masking tape on the cut keeps the plywood from splintering.

Illus. 151. Although cutting the parts to width is easier on a table saw with a rip fence, you can also cut them to width with a portable circular saw.

Illus. 152. If the existing joints in the panel fall in the right spots, they can be reused; otherwise, you'll need to make new joints. Here a rabbet is being cut on the table saw.

shelf, so cut a ¾"-wide by ⅜"-deep dado for the shelf (Illus. 153). While you still have the dado blade set up, make the stopped rabbets for the nailing strip at the top of the cabinet. Lift the board from the saw when the cut is close to the end. Use a chisel to square up the cut (Illus. 154). Base cabinets need a dado for the bottom shelf. The dado can be cut before or after you cut out the space for the toe kick (Illus. 155).

Illus. 153. Dadoes can also be made using the table saw. This dado is for a fixed shelf in the overhead cabinet.

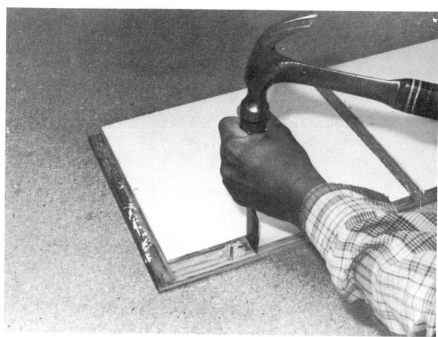

Illus. 154. The nailing strip will be stronger if it is attached with a rabbet joint instead of a butt joint. Make the rabbet with the table saw or a router. Stop the cut when it is close to the correct length; then square it up and bring it to the exact length using a chisel.

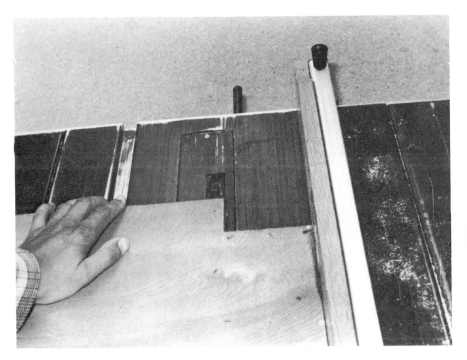

Illus. 155. The bottom shelf in the base cabinet should be attached with a dado. Line up the bottom of the dado with the top of the toe kick so that the front of the shelf will be supported by the toe kick.

When you have all of the parts to size and made the joints, begin to assemble the cabinets. Use glue on all of the joints. Pull the parts together with a bar clamp; then drive finishing nails into the joint (Illus. 156). The nailing strip is particularly important because it will carry the entire weight of overhead cabinets. Make sure that it is securely glued and nailed into the rabbet and along the top (Illus. 157). Base cabinets

Illus. 156. Assemble the cabinet using glue and nails. Use a bar clamp to pull the joints tight as you nail them.

Illus. 157. The nailing strip will carry the weight of overhead cabinets, so make sure that it is securely attached to the sides and top of the carcass.

need a toe kick. The toe kick can be installed in a stopped rabbet, such as the nailing strip, but a simple butt joint is sufficient for most cabinets (Illus. 158).

Put a ¼″-thick plywood or hardboard back in the rabbets and check to see if the cabinet is square. Use a framing square or measure the diagonals from corner to corner. Both diagonals will be equal if the cabinet is

Illus. 158. The toe kick can be attached with a simple butt joint, as shown here, or a rabbet or mitre joint can be used.

square. Use a bar clamp placed diagonally across the corners that are farthest apart to pull the cabinet into square (Illus. 159). Nail the back in place using 3d box nails spaced about 3″ apart.

Install the new cabinets when they are complete. Use clamps to hold the cabinet in position as you drive 3″ dry-wall screws through the nailing strip into the wall studs (Illus. 160). Also, install screws along the bottom of the back to hold the cabinet firmly against the wall. The cabinet in the photo is being placed above the location of the old oven to fill in the area flush with the rest of the overhead cabinets. The base cabinet that was previously used under the cooking top has been moved to fill in the area below the old oven location. A new counter top has

Illus. 159. A bar clamp across the corners of the cabinet can be used to pull a stubbornly out-of-square cabinet into square.

been installed to provide a large uninterrupted work area. The drop-in range fits at the end of this base cabinet, and a small base cabinet was built to fill in the area on the other side of the range.

The worn-out drawer runners were replaced with new plastic guides (Illus. 161) and one additional drawer was built. (See Chapter 7 for details.)

All exposed surfaces of the cabinets are now covered with plastic laminate. The old finish was removed with a belt sander to ensure a smooth surface and good adhesion. Before covering the doors with laminate, they were cut down and a groove was cut in the edge to allow a continuous oak pull to be applied (see Chapter 5). After that, the doors were covered with plastic laminate, following the methods described in Chapter 3.

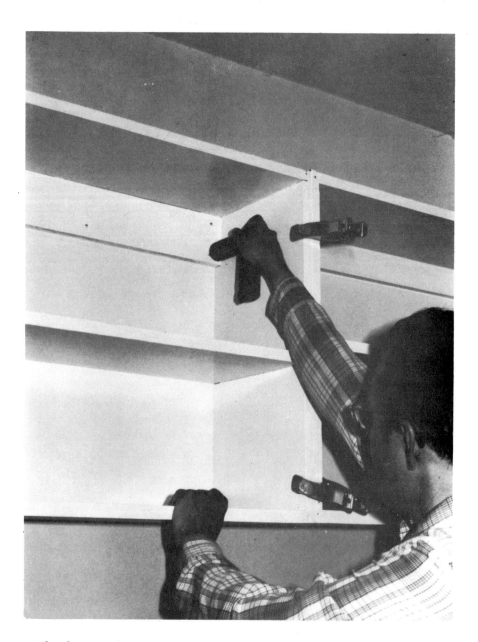

Illus. 160. Before you place the cabinets, find the stud locations. Then clamp the cabinets in place and drive screws through the nailing strip to attach them to the wall.

The hinges that were chosen are meant to be applied to cabinets without face frames. To adapt them to the old sections of the cabinets that had face frames, spacer blocks were installed behind the face frames (Illus. 162). To speed up the marking process, a template similar to the one described in Chapter 5 was used to mark the location of the holes for the hinges (Illus. 163). The drill bit is the correct size for the screws used, and it makes a pilot hole for the 35-mm bit that is used to make the recess in the rear of the door for the cup on the hinge (Illus. 164).

After the hinges are installed on the door and the mounting plates are installed on the cabinets, the doors are lifted into place and the hinges slid onto the mounting plate (Illus. 165). Tightening a set screw attaches

Illus. 161. Wood drawer runners are among the first parts to show signs of wear. In this case, the old runners were replaced with a T-shaped runner and a plastic guide attached to the rear of the drawer. This type of drawer guide was used because it doesn't require any modification to the drawer.

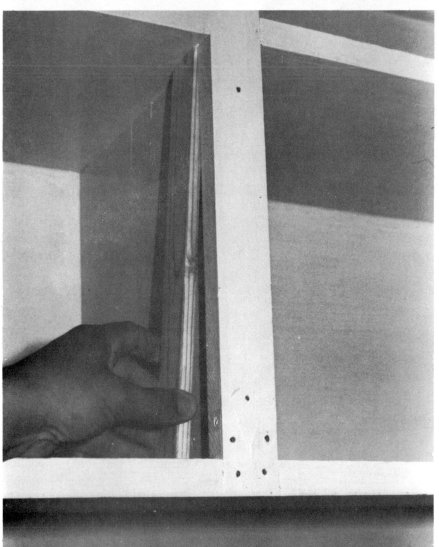

Illus. 162. Spacer blocks installed behind the face frames make it possible to use new hinges designed for cabinets without face frames.

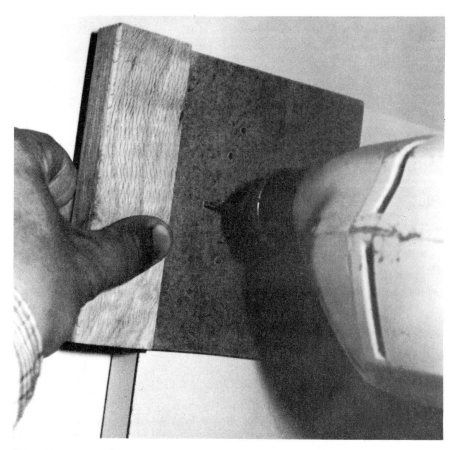

Illus. 163. A template makes it easy to position the holes for the new hinges.

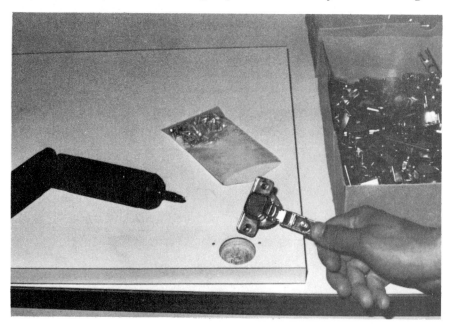

Illus. 164. A 35-mm recess in the door is needed for this type of hinge. The power screwdriver speeds up installation.

the hinge to the plate. When all of the doors are in place, adjust the hinges until the doors line up and the gap between them is uniform.

The completed remodelling makes the old cabinets look like new (Illus. 166). What's more, the plastic-laminate surface will stay new-looking for years and the increased counter space will make the kitchen

Illus. 165. The mounting plates for the hinges are attached to the cabinet before you install the doors. The hinges are attached to the doors; then the doors are attached to the cabinet by sliding the hinges onto the mounting plates and tightening the set screws.

much more usable. The project was completed for about a third of the cost estimated by a contractor for all new cabinets and the labor required to install them. All of the wood for the new cabinets was salvaged from the demolished section except for the ¼″ back. This kept the materials cost low. The major expenses were for plastic laminate and new hinges.

Illus. 166. Even though most of the original materials were reused, the completed remodelling makes the cabinets look and function as if they were new.

METRIC EQUIVALENCY CHART

mm—millimetres   cm—centimetres

INCHES TO MILLIMETRES AND CENTIMETRES

inches	mm	cm	inches	cm	inches	cm
⅛	3	0.3	9	22.9	30	76.2
¼	6	0.6	10	25.4	31	78.7
⅜	10	1.0	11	27.9	32	81.3
½	13	1.3	12	30.5	33	83.8
⅝	16	1.6	13	33.0	34	86.4
¾	19	1.9	14	35.6	35	88.9
⅞	22	2.2	15	38.1	36	91.4
1	25	2.5	16	40.6	37	94.0
1¼	32	3.2	17	43.2	38	96.5
1½	38	3.8	18	45.7	39	99.1
1¾	44	4.4	19	48.3	40	101.6
2	51	5.1	20	50.8	41	104.1
2½	64	6.4	21	53.3	42	106.7
3	76	7.6	22	55.9	43	109.2
3½	89	8.9	23	58.4	44	111.8
4	102	10.2	24	61.0	45	114.3
4½	114	11.4	25	63.5	46	116.8
5	127	12.7	26	66.0	47	119.4
6	152	15.2	27	68.6	48	121.9
7	178	17.8	28	71.1	49	124.5
8	203	20.3	29	73.7	50	127.0

Index